Art and Alienation

Little we see in Nature that is ours. WORDSWORTH

All these consequences flow from the fact that the worker is related to the product of his labour as to an alien thing. KARL MARX

ART AND ALIENATION

The Role of the Artist in Society

HERBERT READ

NEW YORK · THE VIKING PRESS

Contents

A DEFINITION

By alienation is meant a mode of experience in which the person experiences himself as an alien. He has become, one might say, estranged from himself. He does not experience himself as the centre of his world, as the creator of his own acts – but his acts and their consequences have become his masters, whom he obeys, or whom he may even worship. The alienated person is out of touch with himself as he is out of touch with any other person. He, like the others, is experienced as things are experienced; with the senses and with common sense, but at the same time without being related to himself and to the world outside productively. ERICH FROMM *The Sane Society*

Introduction

Art criticism, with notable exceptions in our time such as the work of the Marxist critic, Georg Lukács, has made little attempt to deal with art as a social phenomenon, as a positive factor in the immediate resolution of the problems of contemporary society. It has always seemed, even to Marxist critics, that art is an 'epiphenomenon', something that arises as a consequence of a prevailing economy. I believe that this is a basic error. The aesthetic activity is, on the contrary, a formative process with direct effect both on individual psychology and on social organization. In such a belief I have written most of my books in this sphere – *Art and Society*, *Education through Art*, *The Grass Roots of Art*, *Icon and Idea*, *The Origins of Form in Art*, and now this present volume of essays.

The theory and criticism of art, like any other scientific activity, is based upon the analysis and classification of a specific group of phenomena – works of art. But works of art differ from facts of nature in that their essential characteristics are in no sense measurable. It may be that we are gradually discovering laws of aesthetic evolution, and that the varieties of art can now be classified on lines parallel to Sheldon's classification of the varieties of temperament. But art criticism, even as an academic activity, has shown little consciousness of human psychology, and has remained a hazardous combination of subjective judgement and formal analysis.

An attempt to establish scientific principles of art criticism was made by Heinrich Wölfflin at the beginning of the century – it began with the publication of his *Classic Art* in 1898 and was completed in 1915 with the publication of *Kunstgeschichtliche Grundbegriffe* (*The Principles of Art History*, English translation, 1932). Wölfflin's 'principles' were formalistic, based on the objective analysis of the visual experience of works of art, and with the terminology he provided (a set of five contrary concepts: linear and painterly, plane and recession, closed and open form, multiplicity and unity, absolute and relative clarity), it was found that works of art would yield up the secrets of their composition, and could thus be explained and classified.

Wölfflin's influence was far-reaching, and most of the critics of the first half of this century were submitted to it, notably Berenson and Roger Fry. But at the very moment that Wölfflin was preparing his *Grundbegriffe* the contemporary painters and sculptors were undermining the ground on which he was building. For Wölfflin's principles are based on, and applicable to, one kind of art only– the figurative art of the humanistic tradition. They had no application to earlier traditions such as the Byzantine or the Egyptian; and they have proved to have even less application to various types of modern art.

This is shown in an interesting manner by the disarray caused in the mind of such a sensitive critic as Roger Fry by some of the later phases of the modern movement. Up to a point no one had been so open-minded, so spontaneously sensitive, as Fry. He had welcomed the Fauvists, and introduced the Post-impressionists to England. Cézanne did not give him any trouble (on the contrary, his appreciation of that master remains one of the best available) and he could accept Matisse and Braque, even in their cubist period. He could accept Italians like Severini and Carrà, but for all these artists he had an excuse – they were Latin artists and did not really break with the European tradition of the past– 'their constructions have plastic unity and significance'. But for the later work of Picasso, for the Surrealists and Expressionists, he felt something like physical loathing. 'I must confess', he once wrote, 'that the vast majority of these works leave on my mind a painful impression. I feel that puerility, fatuous self-complacency and sheer bluff, both conscious and unconscious, play a very great part in their production.'[1] He admitted that Klee was 'at least a more consistent artist. He has undoubtedly his own specific, spidery, linear rhythm'. Grudgingly Fry allowed this to be personal and 'expressive', but he went on to attack Klee for being 'the victim of a desire to return to infancy'.

'He reverts to a kind of private picture-writing. He himself gives the clue to this, in a passage called "going for a walk with a line". It would be impossible for anyone to interpret his picture-writing without the clue, so presumably the story which he tells is only his way of arriving at a visually pleasing result, and it is the vision and not the story that matters. The only trouble is that the result is not nearly as interesting or moving *in its formal relations* as the decorations of pots which the modern Indians of New Mexico produce by an exactly similar process of private picture-writing in which every line corresponds, for the artist, to something in his story. But we cannot pretend that even these are more than a rather elementary decorative art, so that we wonder all the more at the vast claims which his admirers make on behalf of the still more elementary efforts of Paul Klee.'

About the same time that he wrote this review Fry was giving his Slade lectures on art at Cambridge, and in the second of these, on 'Sensibility', he returns to Klee, taking the trouble to make a ruled copy of a picture by Klee to demonstrate that 'the design alone manages to express a good deal of his personality. There is his idea of making a figure vaguely symbolic of a human being by this particular arrangement of straight lines, and the wit of abbreviating a figure with parcels into such a form. The proportion of the volumes which the lines are meant to suggest is due to his specific feeling for significant proportions; and the exact position of the figure in the rectangle of the picture is again expressive of his personal choice. But there the story ends.'

Fry then turns to the original picture and admits that it tells us a good deal more than his ruled copy:

'We know that these lines might have been drawn even by the same artist in various ways expressive of different moods. The lines might have been made by vigorous rapid strokes with more or less accent here and there, or they might have been drawn with meticulous care and have approximated more to mechanical exactitude. And if the same figure had been repeated by different artists each one would have declared a different habitual pattern of nervous forces and a variety of that habitual pattern due to the mood in which he drew them. So at once this leads us to distinguish between two aspects of the artist's feeling which are here clearly represented by the two images before you. One is the feeling expressed by the artist in his design, in the planning and the proportion of the parts to the whole; and the other is the feeling expressed by the artist in executing that design.'[2]

In this passage Fry is trying to escape from the impasse into which a formalistic method of criticism had led him, but he does not really succeed. He had discovered that Wölfflin's formal relations were not the whole story of art, and though he still tries to make them account for the effectiveness of the design itself, he has to allow for an informal element which he calls the artist's sensibility, the 'surface sensibility'. 'We are, as it were, forced to abandon our intellectual in favour of our sensual logic.' But for Fry the whole process of criticism (or appreciation) remains a 'logic', a process that can be explained by reason. Klee's own explanation of the process of art and of his own intentions was very different. There is a passage in his lecture *On Modern Art* which might have been written with Fry's criticism in mind – it was, as a matter of fact, written ten years earlier:

'The legend of the childishness of my drawing must have originated from those linear compositions of mine in which I tried to combine a concrete image, say that of a man, with the pure representation of the linear element.

Had I wished to present the man "as he is", then I should have had to use such a bewildering confusion of line that pure elementary representation would have been out of the question. The result would have been vagueness beyond recognition.

And anyway, I do not wish to represent the man as he is, but only as he might be.

And thus I could arrive at a happy association between my vision of life (*Weltanschauung*) and pure artistic craftsmanship.'[3]

Klee would have been the last to deny the importance of formal relations or of sensibility, but he saw these as means towards an end – as the elements of a language which had to express an order of reality, as symbols of great evocative power. Fry remained a sensationalist – even a materialist; but Klee was a symbolist – even a transcendentalist. In that distinction lies the whole difference between two ways of art, two methods of art criticism.

There is nothing new in the notion of symbolic art, and even criticism, before Wölfflin and other German art historians and psychologists came along, was often an exercise in symbolic interpretation. Ruskin was a symbolic critic, insisting that we should first *see* the work of art, and then *read* it. Baudelaire was a symbolic critic, and so was Pater. In fact, all criticism that was ever worth anything, and that has survived its brief day of topical relevance, was symbolic in this sense, taking the work of art as a symbol to be interpreted, rather than as an object to be dissected. But interpretation, if it is to be regarded as a method of criticism, requires more definition than the recital of these few names provides.

Obviously interpretative criticism must be basically a subjective activity. The plastic symbols of art express feelings or intuitions which are unique – they cannot be given an exact translation into words, though we may think that Pater's description of Botticelli's *Birth of Venus*, or Ruskin's description of Turner's *Slave Ship*, are very near equivalents. The most we can say is that interpretation will approach to an exact translation of experience the more nearly one art (the art of words) is substituted for another art (the art of plastic images). It is perhaps significant that the best interpretative critics – Diderot, Hazlitt, Ruskin, Baudelaire, Fromentin, Pater – have all been good writers, independently of their art criticism. The very faculties which go to make a good writer – sensuousness, sympathy, energy – are also the faculties needed for the appreciation of the plastic arts. One sees the equivocation beautifully displayed in both Ruskin and Baudelaire, even in Hazlitt. In such artists there is a hesitation, sometimes continuing for many years, between the careers of painter and writer. The role of the poet as the midwife of painting has been

illustrated in our half-century by Guillaume Apollinaire and
André Breton. These are the true critics, the critics who matter
to the artist because they sympathize and encourage, electrify
and fight. Those who follow up in the rear, hiding their timid
steps under their academic gowns, hoping to find a dead corpse
or two on the way to dissect – these are critics of the second rank,
camp followers. Usually they arrive too late even to celebrate
a victory.

But I do not wish to imply that interpretative criticism must
be practised exclusively by poets. A basic sensibility is necessary,
but the more the critic supports this by logical disciplines the
better. I am thinking in particular of logic itself, or of what used
to be called rhetoric – the science of effective statement. Between
the intuitive understanding of a work of art and the communication of this understanding to the public lies a mental process of
translation with its rules, sometimes known as hermeneutics.
This probably amounts to no more than insisting that the critic
should play fair, and not substitute his own symbols and metaphors for those intended by the artist. This warning is necessary
because it has become quite feasible, with the implied support
of Freud and Jung, to substitute for the painter's symbols (precise
plastic images that they be) another set of symbols with quite
a different context – erotic, mythic, archetypal. I am not suggesting that a psycho-analytical approach to a work of art is unjusti-
fied; apart from the many illuminating asides (they are hardly
more than that) which Freud and Jung have thrown out about
specific works of art, there are a few direct applications of the
method that are genuinely interpretative. A good example is
Juan Larrea's essay on Picasso's *Guernica*, published in 1947 by
Curt Valentin in New York. *Guernica* is often regarded, not only
as Picasso's masterpiece, but also as the most socially significant
painting of the half-century. Before such a symbolic vision a
formalistic criticism can only utter ineptitudes. A poet might
conceivably have created an equivalent myth – Lorca might have
done so if he had been spared. But short of such a *poetic* interpretation, Larrea's psychological treatment alone is adequate. But
Larrea's intention is not coldly clinical – he does not murder his
subject to dissect it, but shows us the life, individual and collective,

vibrating in every line of Picasso's composition. One might object to a certain unscientific rhetoric, did it not express the truth, which is that this painting 'is the beginning of a new pictorial era':

'For when there is an end to the pitiless deluge of fire which has levelled to the ground the buildings of the ancient world, we shall see, outlined at the horizon, a new alliance of Heaven and Earth; within the pregnant round of the rainbow, a new Phoenix is preparing a rebirth in peace from the ashes to which *Guernica* has reduced all that was dead in painting.' (*Plates 1, 2*)

And all that was dead in criticism! It will still take some time for art criticism to discard its formalistic habits, and to emerge in free and sympathetic collaboration with the symbolic intentions of the modern artist. What still remains to be done is to show the social relevance of these symbolic modes of representation, and to do this despite the opposition of those politically minded critics whose conception of art is limited to realism – to the superficial ideal of the bourgeoisie of the nineteenth century.

The essays collected in this volume were written on various occasions, but they all revert sooner or later to the central theme of the alienated artist. Part One consists of general essays that deal with the situation of the artist in a world dominated by science and technology. The essays that follow in Part Two discuss individual artists, and among these I have included two or three artists of the past, partly to show that our problems are not peculiar to contemporary society. It is perhaps more difficult to justify the inclusion of the essays on Vermeer and Matisse because they would seem to be artists completely untouched by the problems of alienation. But I present them as artists who have solved these problems, artists who have achieved an ideal of 'luxe, calme et volupté'. The possibility of alienation exists whenever social and political developments create feelings of anxiety and despair, of rootlessness and insecurity, of isolation and apathy. Life itself is tragic, and a profound art always begins with this realization. In the past it was still possible for the alienated artist to address his fellow-men in a traditional language of symbolic forms, but to have lost this advantage is the peculiar fate of the modern artist: a *lingua franca* of visual symbols no longer exists. For this reason there may be a qualitative difference between the alienation of modern artists and the alienation of artists such as Bosch and Grünewald. Never before in the history of our Western world has the divorce between man and nature, between man and his fellow-men, between individual man and his 'self-hood' been so complete. Such is one of the main effects of that system of production we call capitalism, as Marx foresaw. We now realize that not capitalism alone, but the whole character and scope of a technological civilization is involved (the end of capitalism in certain countries has not meant the end of alienation). To change the world, meaning the prevailing economic system, is not enough. The fragmented psyche must be reconstituted, and only the creative therapy we call art offers that possibility.

PART ONE

I

The Function of the Arts in Contemporary Society

'Art' and 'Society' are two of the vaguest concepts in modern language – I say *modern* language because these words have no exact equivalents in the ancient European languages, which are much more concrete in their terminology. In the English language the word 'art' is so ambiguous that no two people will spontaneously define it in the same sense. Sophisticated people will try to isolate some characteristic common to all the arts – they then find themselves involved in the science of art, in aesthetics, finally in metaphysics. Simple people tend to identify art with one of the arts, usually painting. They are confused if they are asked to consider music or architecture as art. Common to both sophisticated and simple people is the assumption that whatever art may be, it is a specialist or professional activity of no direct concern of the average man.

Society is equally vague as a concept. A society may mean the total inhabitants of a country – it may even mean mankind as a whole. At the opposite extreme it may mean a few people who have come together for a common but special purpose – the members of a religious sect or a club. But just as we have a science of art which tries to bring order to a confused subject, so we have a science of society, sociology, which tries to give logical coherence to this second concept. The two sciences, aesthetics and sociology, rarely overlap, but there have been attempts to create a sociology of art, and various utopias, and works such as Plato's

Politicus, are concerned with an art of society, with government or social organization conceived as an art rather than as a science.

Very few philosophers, though Plato is one of them, have seen that art and society are inseparable concepts – that society, as a viable organic entity, is somehow dependent on art as a binding, fusing and energizing force. That has always been my own view of the relationship, and in this essay I should like to give some account of what such a relationship involves (or has involved in the past) and of the fatal consequences of the absence of any such relationship in our contemporary civilization.

Both art and society in any concrete sense of the terms have their origin in man's relation to his natural environment. The earliest surviving works of art are the fairly numerous Palaeolithic cave-paintings and a few figurines in bone or ivory of the same period. We have no precise knowledge of the origins or purpose of these works of art, but no one supposes that they were works of art for art's sake. They may have had a magical or a religious function and as such were intimately related to the social structure of that time. This is also true of the art of all the succeeding civilizations of which we have historical evidence. If we examine the first records of the early civilizations of Sumer, Egypt or the Middle East, we always find artifacts that still appeal to our aesthetic sensibility – indeed, our knowledge of these societies is largely based on the evidence derived from surviving works of art.

All the way down the long perspective of history it is impossible to conceive of a society without art, or of an art without social significance, until we come to the modern epoch. Sparta is sometimes given as an exception, but this view depends on a narrow interpretation of art: Xenophon regarded the Spartan cosmos as in itself a work of art.[1] As for a tribe such as the Philistines, which by a strange chance has become identified with all that is insensitive and barbaric in society, it was probably as artistic as any other militant society of its time: it is said to have had a nice taste in feather head-dresses. It should be noted that Matthew Arnold, who gave general currency to Philistinism as a term of contempt, meant by it inaccessibility to *ideas*, and not specifically a lack of aesthetic sensibility, though he implied that only in so far as a society is permeated by ideas and vivified by them does it rise to the proper appreciation of art.[2] My own inclination is to reverse the statement: only in so far as a society is rendered sensitive by the arts do ideas become accessible to it.

We may next ask how does it come about that modern societies have become insensitive to the arts. The hypothesis that at once suggests itself is that this fundamental change is, in some sense to be determined, a consequence of the sudden increase in the size of societies, a development that accompanies the industrialization of a country. It has always been a matter for wonder that the greatest epochs of art – Athens in the seventh and sixth centuries B. C., Western Europe in the twelfth and thirteenth centuries, the city-states of Italy in the fourteenth and fifteenth centuries, are associated with communities that, in comparison with the typical modern state, were minuscule. We tend to ignore this fact, to regard it as irrelevant, and even to assume that the biggest and most powerful nations must naturally, in due course, produce the greatest art. It is a conclusion for which history offers no support.

The most cursory consideration of the nature of the creative process in the arts will give us the explanation of this paradox. Whatever may be the nature of the relationship between art and society, the work of art itself is always the creation of an individual. It is true that there are arts, such as drama, the dance and ritual, that are complex by nature and depend on a group of individuals for their execution or presentation; nevertheless, the unity that gives force and singularity and effectiveness to any one example of these arts is the creative intuition of a particular dramatist, choreographer or architect. There are, of course, many examples of effective collaboration in the arts, but, to use one of Coleridge's neologisms, they are always 'coadunitive': they consist of separate individual contributions, joined together like 'a quarter of an orange, a quarter of an apple, and the like of a lemon and a pomegranate', and made to look like 'one round diverse fruit'. Coleridge's metaphor is used to distinguish between the talents of Beaumont and Fletcher and the genius of Shakespeare. Similarly, I have yet to be convinced that any project realized by an 'architects co-operative', for example, can have the aesthetic value of a work conceived by an individual architect. Sentimental medievalists used to suggest that the Gothic cathedral was a communal creation, but this is to confuse building and design: all that was significant and original in any particular Gothic cathedral was 'the singular expression of a singular experience', and though architecture, if it is of any complexity, always involves the employment of subsidiary executants, builders and craftsmen, the aesthetic concept, that is to say, the work conceived as an artistic unity, is always the product of an individual vision and sensibility.[3]

But the individual does not work in a vacuum. The whole complexity of our problem arises from the fact that the artist is in some sense dependent on the community, not merely in the obvious economic sense, but in a sense that is far subtler, and waiting for psychological analysis. I do not propose to attempt such an analysis: indeed, I doubt if even the science of social psychology is advanced enough to enable us to formulate a definite hypothesis on this subject. What is required is an analysis that would define two separate but interacting psychic entities: on the one hand the subjective ego of the artist, seeking to adjust itself to the external world of nature and society; on the other hand, society itself as an organism with its own laws of internal and external adjustment (we speak of 'crowd psychology'). Herein lies one of the basic paradoxes of human existence: art is the pattern evolved in a complex interplay of personal and societal processes of adjustment. It is only possible on the present occasion to give a brief description of this problematic situation.

Perhaps I should begin by indicating certain evasions of the problem. The first is the one that most directly concerns an international organization such as UNESCO, but it is found in most democratic countries, that is to say, in all those that have become aware of the problem. An awareness of the problem arises in the following way and for the following reasons. It is realized that art as a social activity has characterized the great social systems of the past, from prehistoric and primitive civilizations to the great aristocratic, ecclesiastic and oligarchic societies of more recent times. This inevitable and apparently significant association of art and society is then seen to break down with the inception of the modern age – the age of industrialization, mass production, population explosion and parliamentary democracy.

Two deductions are then possible. The first, which prevailed generally during the nineteenth century, assumes that art is a thing of the past, and that a civilization such as ours can dispense with it. The second deduction, which is more and more characteristic of our own time, denies this historicist assumption, asserts that what is wrong with our present civilization can be diagnosed, and proceeds to recommend various remedies.

I shall for the moment ignore the historicist point of view, for which Hegel was originally responsible, and examine some of the policies whose aim is to remedy the existing situation.

The most popular and in my opinion the most ineffective of these remedies is economic subsidy. It is pointed out, quite truly, that art in the past always had its patrons – the Church in the Middle Ages, the Princes and City Councils of the Renaissance, the Merchants of the seventeenth and eighteenth centuries. This is a superficial generalization that would not survive a scientific analysis – there is no demonstrable connection between the quality of art in any period and the quantity of patronage: patrons for the most part have been whimsical, inconsistent and sometimes positively tasteless or reactionary. But there is no need to examine this explanation of the present situation because the patronage at present enjoyed by the arts is probably greater in amount than at any previous time in European history. In the past fifty years vast sums have been expended on the purchase not only of 'old masters' but also of contemporary works of art of all schools, and equally large sums have been spent on the building of museums, theatres, opera houses, concert halls, etc., and on the subsidy of performances in such institutions. All to no effect on the basic problem, which is the creation of a vital democratic art to correspond to our democratic civilization. Our civilization, in its visual aspects, is chaotic; it is without a characteristic poetry, without a typical drama: its painting and sculpture have now sunk to a level of mindless incoherence whilst its architecture is reduced to an 'economic' functionalism that projects its own 'brutalism' as an aesthetic virtue. There are exceptions to these generalizations, but nowhere in the world today is there a *style* of art that springs spontaneously from the basic social and economic realities of our way of life.

The first question to ask and the most profoundly disturbing one is whether there is an incompatibility between those basic realities (our system of economic production) and the spontaneous production of works of art. Before answering that question it is perhaps necessary to affirm that there is no change in the potentiality of the human race for the production of works of art. Again I am evading Hegel's suggestion that art, 'on the side of its highest possibilities' (an important qualification) is a thing of the past. I proceed on the assumption that human nature, *in its potentialities*, does not change (or has not changed within measurable time). The world is full of frustrated artists, or rather, of people whose creative instincts have been frustrated. Burckhardt, whom I intend to quote more than once in the course of this essay, pointed out that *'there may now exist great men for things that do not exist'*. I refer not only to obvious geniuses who in spite of the times they live in give evidence of their genius in fragmented works of individualistic expressionism – the works of artists such as Picasso, Klee, Schönberg, Stravinsky, Pasternak, Eliot – but also to all those potential artists who waste their talents in so-called commercial art (a contradiction in terms) and to all those sensitive children who give early proof of their potentialities and are then sacrificed like rams on the altars of industrial expedience. One of the most tragic injustices of our technological civilization is that the natural sensibility of men which in other ages found an outlet in basic crafts is now completely suppressed, or finds a pathetic outlet in some trivial 'hobby'.

I begin, therefore, by affirming with Burckhardt, that 'the arts are a faculty of man, a power and a creation. Imagination, their vital, central impulse, has at all times been regarded as divine'. It is true that we must always distinguish (as Burckhardt does) between the doers and the seers, between the craftsmen and the visionaries. 'To give tangible form to that which is inward, to represent it in such a way that we see it as the outward image of inward things – that is a most rare power. To re-create the external in external form – that is within the power of many.'[4]

We must examine our way of life – our social structure, our methods of production and distribution, the accumulation of capital and the incidence of taxation, to decide whether it is not in these factors that we should look for an explanation of our aesthetic impotence. To do this in detail would be a task for a separate book, not a brief essay, but I have written much on the subject in the past and would now only point briefly to two or three characteristics of our civilization which are patently inimical to the arts.

1. The first is the general phenomenon of *alienation* which has been much written about since Hegel invented the term and Marx gave it political significance. The term is used to denote both a social and a psychological problem, but these are but two aspects of the same problem, the essence of which is the progressive divorce of human faculties from natural processes. Apart from the many social aspects of the problem (beginning with the division of labour and leading to the elimination of labour or automation, and other consequences of the industrial revolution such as conurbation and congestion, disease and delinquency) there is a general effect, noticed by social philosophers such as Ruskin and Thoreau, but not greatly the concern of 'scientific' sociologists, which might be described as the atrophy of sensibility. If seeing and handling, touching and hearing and all the refinements of sensation that developed historically in the conquest of nature and the manipulation of material substances are not educed and trained from birth to maturity the result is a being that hardly deserves to be called human: a dull-eyed, bored and listless automaton whose one desire is for violence in some form or other – violent action, violent sounds, distractions of any kind that can penetrate to its deadened nerves. Its preferred distractions are: the sports stadium, the pin-table alleys, the dance-hall, the passive 'viewing' of crime, farce and sadism on the television screen, gambling and drug addiction.

2. The decline of religious worship is doubtless the inevitable consequence of a growth of scientific rationalism, and the fact that scientific progress has not been accompanied by any equivalent progress in ethical standards is frequently regretted. But it is not so often observed that the same forces that have destroyed the mystery of holiness have destroyed the mystery of beauty. To quote Burckhardt again:

'. . . from the beginning of time, we find the artists and poets in solemn and great relationship with religion and culture ... they alone can interpret and give imperishable form to the mystery of beauty. Everything that passes by us in life, so swift, rare and unequal, is here gathered together in a world of poems, in pictures and great picture-cycles, in colour, stone and sound, to form a second, sublime world on earth. Indeed, in architecture and music we can only experience beauty through art; without art we should not know that it exists.'5 But more than this: without art we should not know that truth exists, for truth is only made visible, apprehensible and acceptable in the work of art.

I am not suggesting that this process of rationalization is reversible: the mind never gives up its materialistic conquests, short of world catastrophe. I am merely pointing to the obvious fact that the scope of scientific knowledge is still limited. The nature of the cosmos and the origins and purpose of human life remain as mysteries, and this means that science has by no means replaced the symbolic functions of art, which are still necessary 'to overcome the resistance of the brutish world'.

3. Thirdly, and most diffidently, one must mention a characteristic of our way of life which however solidly based on our cherished ideals of democracy is inimical to art. I have already mentioned the obvious fact that works of art are produced by individuals. It follows from this that the values of art are essentially aristocratic: they are not determined by a general level of aesthetic sensibility, but by the best aesthetic sensibility available at any particular time. This is a faculty possessed by relatively few people – the arbiters of taste, the critics and connoisseurs and, above all, artists themselves – and the level of taste is determined by their intercourse. Whatever we may think of Carlyle's or Burckhardt's theory of the role of the great man in history – and Burckhardt pointed out that there are many categories of great men, some of them of doubtful benefit to humanity – and however much importance we may give to 'the grass roots' theory of art, a theory which I have frequently expounded and to which without paradox I remain faithful – nevertheless, the history of art is a graph traced between points which represent the appearance in history of a great artist. A Michelangelo or a Mozart may be the product of ascertainable forces, hereditary

or social; but once he has created his works of art, the history of art departs from its previous course. I do not, of course, assume that the history of art is identical with the history of culture. Culture is not even the sum of all the arts, or of all the arts, customs, scientific and religious beliefs of a period. As T. S. Eliot once pointed out, all these parts into which a culture can be analysed act upon each other and a culture is something they create which is greater than the sum of their parts. Fully to understand one art you have to understand all. Nevertheless, 'there are of course higher cultures, and the higher cultures in general are distinguished by differentiation of function, so that you can speak of the less cultured and the more cultured strata of society, and finally, you speak of individuals as being exceptionally cultured. The culture of an artist or a philosopher is distinct from that of a mine worker or field labourer; the culture of a poet will be somewhat different from that of a politician; but in a healthy society these are all parts of the same culture; and the artist, the poet, the philosopher, the politician and the labourer will have a culture in common, which they do not share with other people of the same occupations in other countries.'[6]

Unfortunately for art, a democratic society has its own categories of greatness which do not necessarily correspond to our definitions of culture. I do not refer so much to the heroes of war, politics or sport. These non-aesthetic categories are common to all ages. I confine my observations to the arts and in this sphere modern democracy has shown a total incapacity to distinguish between genius and talents. This is probably due to the strangeness or originality of genius – even in other ages, genius was not always immediately recognized at its true worth. But more recently technological advances in methods of communication have conspired with an innate envy of originality to produce that typical famous man of our time, the pander. Whether as a columnist or a television 'personality', this usurper appears before a public numbering millions and by anticipating their opinions and prejudices, flatters them into concurrence and adulation. To see – actually to see – their own commonplace thoughts and instinctive judgements voiced by an eloquent Jack-in-a-box not merely gives people the illusion that greatness is democratic, but also the greater illusion that truth need not be disturbing. For complacency (allied to complicity) is the ultimate ideal of a democratic way of life.

Art, on the other hand, is eternally disturbing, permanently revolutionary. It is so because the artist, in the degree of his greatness, always confronts the unknown, and what he brings back from that confrontation is a novelty, a new symbol, a new vision of life, the outer image of inward things. His importance to society is not that he voices received opinions, or gives clear expression to the confused feelings of the masses: that is the function of the politician, the journalist, the demagogue. The artist is what the Germans call *ein Rüttler*, an upsetter of the established order. The greatest enemy of art is the collective mind, in any of its many manifestations. The collective mind is like water that always seeks the lowest level of gravity: the artist struggles out of this morass, to seek a higher level of individual sensibility and perception. The signals he sends back are often unintelligible to the multitude, but then come the philosophers and critics to interpret his message. On the basic works of one genius, a Homer, a Plato, a Dante, a Shakespeare, a Michelangelo, a Bach or Mozart we build, not only outworks of interpretation and explication, but also extensions and imitations, until the art of one individual pervades and gives name to an epoch. These concrete achievements in the plastic arts are the basis for what Hegel called 'reflective culture'. In admitting that the true function of art is 'to bring to consciousness the highest interests of mind', he was contradicting his previous statement that art is a thing of the past. For to 'bring to consciousness' is a process of reification, of concretization, that is or should be continuous in history. 'The imagination *creates*', as Hegel admitted; art does not deal in thoughts, but in 'the real external forms of what exists', with the raw material of Nature. Writing in the 1820s, in the full flood of the Romantic movement, and before the effects of the industrial revolution had been felt, Hegel might well conclude that European art had come to the end of its task and had created more than the mind of the coming century could digest; but he was spared the experience of an age that can deny the very functions of imagination, genius, and inspiration.

From whatever angle we approach this problem of the function of the arts in contemporary society, it is evident that their proper function is inhibited by the nature of that society. The Hegelian contradiction between art and idea loses its force and application in a society that has no use for either – neither for 'the soul and its emotions' nor for 'a concrete sensuous phenomenon', the two dialectical entities which in a progressive civilization are fused into unity by the *vital energy* that is life itself in its creative evolution.

It may be said that I have placed my priorities in the wrong order (actually I am denying that there are any priorities in the process). It has been generally assumed, at least in my own country where Matthew Arnold gave currency to the opinion, that 'the exercise of the creative power in the production of great works of literature or art . . . is not at all epochs and under all conditions possible . . . the elements with which the creative power works are ideas; the best ideas . . . current at the time.'[7] Arnold limits his illustrations to literature, but his meaning is quite general. 'The grand work of literary genius is a work of synthesis and exposition, not of analysis or discovery; its gift lies in the faculty of being happily inspired by a certain intellectual and spiritual atmosphere, by a certain order of ideas, when it finds itself in them; of dealing divinely with these ideas, presenting them in the most effective and attractive combinations – making beautiful works with them, in short.'[8] This is the intellectualist heresy derived no doubt from Goethe and indirectly from Hegel. While it is true that in the creation of a master-work (in any of the arts) 'two powers must concur, the power of the man and the power of the moment', the essence of any work of art does not lie in synthesis and exposition, nor even in analysis and discovery, but in realization and manifestation. What is realized is an image – 'we must render the image of what we see, forgetting everything that existed before us' (Cézanne). The artist, whether he is a poet or a painter, a musician or a potter, *gives concrete shape to sensations and perceptions*' (Cézanne again); and what he manifests is this *shape*, in colours, in words, in sounds. The rest is what Wittgenstein called 'the language game', and has nothing to do with art.

But that manifested shape is the node from which in due course ideas spring, and the more precise, the more vital the work of art, the more powerful will be the ideas it suggests. Then we can say with Arnold that 'the touch of truth is the touch of life, and there is a stir and growth everywhere'. But the first necessity is that the artist should render the image; if there are no images there are no ideas, and a civilization slowly but inevitably dies.

I believe that there is only one way of saving our civilization and that is by so reforming its constituent societies that, in the sense of the phrases already defined, the concrete sensuous phenomena of art are once more spontaneously manifested in our daily lives. I have called this reform 'education through art' and it now has advocates throughout the world. But what I have not sufficiently emphasized, and what is not sufficiently realized by many of my fellow-workers in this field, is the revolutionary nature of the remedy. An education through art is not necessarily anti-scientific, for science itself depends on the clear manifestation of concrete sensuous phenomena, and is necessarily impeded by 'the language game'. But an education through art does not fit human beings for the mindless and mechanical actions of modern industry; it does not reconcile them to a leisure devoid of constructive purpose; it does not leave them satisfied with passive entertainment. It aims to create 'stir and growth' everywhere, to substitute for conformity and imitation in each citizen an endowment of imaginative power 'in a kind perfectly unborrowed and his own' (Coleridge).

What practical alternative is anywhere suggested? Only in China have I seen any awareness of the supreme importance of the problem of alienation, which they attempt to solve, not by an education through art, but by insisting that an education is not complete that does not include some direct contact with nature, a basic exercise of the senses in the bitter struggle to win subsistence from the soil. Such a policy takes the citizen back to the point where civilization is born, and heals the wound which we have called alienation. If such a policy succeeds in reuniting the divided psyche of man, a vital energy will once more begin to flow from sensation to feeling, from imagination to mind. But as things are at present, this precious stream will remain at the mercy of ideologists, to be dammed and diverted to the fulfilment of their materialistic aims. Alas, in the end we have to admit with Burckhardt that what every nation desires, implicitly or explicitly, is power, and that the fragmentation of power, the diminution of size, which history has shown to be the organic scale for cultural vitality, is now regarded as a sign of weakness, a brand of shame. 'The individual cannot find any satisfaction in such a service; his one desire is to participate in a great entity, and this clearly betrays power as the primary and culture as a very secondary goal at best. More specifically, the idea is to make the general will of the nation felt abroad, in defiance of other nations. Hence, firstly, the hopelessness of any attempt at decentralization, of any voluntary restriction of power in favour of local and civilized life. The central will can never be too strong.'⁹

It will be said that these gloomy prognostications have been contradicted by the cultural achievements of modern powers such as the British Commonwealth, the United States of America, the Union of Socialist Soviet Republics. But has there been, in any sense remotely comparable to the cultures of Athens, Rome, Florence or Holland, Mexico, Japan, a British culture, an American culture, a Russian culture? An empire is by definition a power-concept; art is born in intimacy.

This is not a quietist philosophy; there is no necessary association between art and inactivity. It is true that at the practical level there is a general contradiction between extrovert activities and the calm needed for creative work of any kind. War and revolution destroy the constructive works of the artist. But at the same time we must admit with Burckhardt that 'passion is the mother of great things'. The artist is stimulated by great events, even although he takes no part in them and does not even celebrate them directly in his works. What matters is the general atmosphere of vitality 'when unsuspected forces awake in individuals and even heaven takes on a different hue' – or as Wordsworth expresses the sentiment in a famous passage of *The Prelude* inspired by the French Revolution:

> O pleasant exercise of hope and joy!
> For mighty were the auxiliars which then stood
> Upon our side, we who were strong in love!

> Bliss was it in that dawn to be alive,
> But to be young was very heaven! O times,
> In which the meagre, stale, forbidding way
> Of custom, law, and statute, took at once
> The attraction of a country in romance! . . .
> Not favoured spots alone, but the whole earth
> The beauty wore of promise – that which sets . . .
> The budding rose above the rose full blown.[10]

Unfortunately the artist is not always destined to live in such a dawn or, having lived in it, not often destined to contemplate it in the tranquillity of some safe retreat. Great poets and painters appeared in the dawn of the Russian Revolution, but they were destined to perish miserably.

There are few conclusions in this field that can claim scientific validity. Genius is a genetic chance and history a confused clamour, but life persists. It is a flame that rises and sinks, now flickers and now burns steadily, and the source of the oil that feeds it is invisible. But that source is always associated with the imagination, and a civilization like our own that consistently denies or destroys the life of the imagination must inevitably sink into deeper and deeper barbarism.

II

Rational Society and Irrational Art

Explanations of the place and function of art in society offered by sociologists are so multifarious and contradictory that a mere philosopher of art like myself tends to fall back on formalism as the only logical basis for a discussion of the subject. It is true that such tactics involve a redefinition of form, but this has in any case been made necessary by our expanding knowledge of the many varieties of art prevailing in the past and manifested in our own time. This revolution in aesthetics has not been a concession to external influences such as those of social science or technology, but rather a recognition of the fact that a philosophy of art based on the evidence provided by the Graeco-Roman tradition is no longer adequate to account for the aesthetic values of quite other traditions, such as the Oriental, the African, the Pre-Columbian, nor can it account for those new traditions, partly inspired by the discovery of exotic art, to which we give the generic name of 'modernism'.

All these separate traditions can, of course, be *described* in terms of climatic conditions, of economic and social structure, but description is not explanation and art remains a distinct entity, often, as Marx realized, in flagrant opposition to the norms of economic production. This opposition can be interpreted in Hegelian terms as alienation, and this, for the art of the past, is the interpretation favoured by Herbert Marcuse. Literature and art were devised (consciously or unconsciously) as a cover for the contradictions of a divided world – 'the defeated possibilities, the hopes unfulfilled, and the promises betrayed'.

Let us accept for the moment this description of the art of the past, merely noting in passing the emphasis on form. Marcuse then proceeds to an original and contentious statement about the art of our present technological era. 'The developing technological reality undermines not only the traditional forms but the very basis of the artistic alienation – that is, it tends to invalidate not only certain "styles" but also the very substance of art.' In accordance with the general trend of 'one-dimensional society', 'in the realm of culture, the new totalitarianism manifests itself precisely in a harmonizing pluralism, where the most contradictory works and truths peacefully co-exist in indifference'. Even the traditional images of artistic alienation, the 'classics' of the past, are, so to speak, de-alienated – they are 'incorporated into this society and circulate as part and parcel of the equipment which adorns and psychoanalyses the prevailing state of affairs. Thus they become commercials – they sell, comfort, or excite.' And coming to life as other than themselves 'they are deprived of their antagonistic force, of the estrangement which was the very dimension of their truth.'[1]

I do not wish to question this analysis of what is actually happening in our society. As culture is popularized, is 'mediated' to the masses, it is necessarily diluted, castrated, de-formed (in the precise sense that the form the artist gave to his work is destroyed in order to comply with the technological demands of the medium, whether film or radio, and with the supposed 'level of appreciation' for which these media cater). As a consequence of this 'process of technological rationality' the whole basis of aesthetic judgement is subtly perverted and the pre-technological images lose their power.

This change is particularly noticeable in academic circles, where the masterpieces of the past are not so much subject to re-evaluation – a process which is always necessary on other, namely, aesthetic grounds – as dismissed as no longer relevant in a technological society. I have myself in the past called for a revaluation of the art of the past on the basis of the new aesthetic values – for example, in an essay on 'Surrealism and the Romantic Principle'.[2]

I even proposed that such a revaluation should be based on Hegel's dialectics! But it is one thing to question traditional aesthetic judgements on the grounds that they have become *conventional*, that is to say, no longer organically aesthetic, and quite another thing to question such judgements on grounds that are extra-aesthetic – namely social, political, moral or technological. The work of art, the intellectual function of form apart, is always a physical syndrome – it exists within a complex of emotion and feeling, and for its proper appreciation it may demand selective channels of communication – a fact which Marcuse fully recognizes. But when an academic critic, a professor of English Literature in one of the new English universities, tells us that the poetry of Shelley is no longer viable[3] one suspects he is merely asserting that Shelley's images are pre-technological: in other words, since technological man is already 'good, great and joyous, beautiful and free' he no longer needs

> To suffer woes which Hope thinks infinite;
> To forgive wrongs darker than death or night;
>   To defy Power, which seems omnipotent;
> To love, and bear; to hope till Hope creates
> From its own wreck the thing it contemplates . . .

Suffering and forgiveness, love and hope are part of the terminology of estrangement and the images associated with such feelings have lost their power because technological man no longer has such feelings.[4] He does not suffer so how can he forgive; he does not love and therefore has no need to hope.

Herbert Marcuse seems to accept the possibility that the physical transformation of the world entails the mental transformation of man's symbols, images, and ideas, but 'since contradiction is the work of the Logos' (a gnomic utterance I do not quite understand) he concludes that a technological culture must have its own medium of communication. 'The struggle for this medium, or rather the struggle against its absorption into the predominant one-dimensionality, shows forth in the avant-garde efforts to create an estrangement which would make the artistic truth again communicable.' In other words, since art demands for its vitality a condition of estrangement, and since our one-dimensional society does not provide such a condition, it must be artificially created (or imagined).

To what extent does contemporary art exhibit such a tendency? Marcuse relies on Brecht as a conscious exponent of such an artificial *Verfremdungseffekt*. According to Marcuse, Brecht's *Schriften zum Theater* reveal him as consciously aware of the need for mental conflict as a basis for art. The things of everyday must be lifted out of the realm of the self-evident – 'That which is "natural" must assume the features of the extraordinary. Only in this manner can the laws of cause and effect reveal themselves.'[5] On such grounds not only the work of Brecht, but the whole 'theatre of the absurd' can be justified in a rational society. Even the whole Surrealist movement, which is not so *passé* as some of its critics assume (it died as a movement when it became acceptable as a social phenomenon, that is to say, when it was absorbed into the predominant one-dimensionality), has been comfortably adapted to our technological culture – witness the 'surreality' of the James Bond films. But the process, Marcuse points out, is one of 'desublimation'. The aim of tragic art of the past was a sublimation of the instincts – 'mediated gratification' or catharsis. Replace this effect by immediate gratification and the whole exercise loses its point. The tragedy becomes a farce.

Everything in Brecht's theatre, observes one of Brecht's most perceptive critics,[6] 'is dedicated to the same end: replacing a magical theatre with a scientific one, a childish theatre with an adult one'. Admirable as this may be as a social ideal, it is not a possible ideal for art: art is basically irrational and even infantile, and to require the artist, as does Brecht (and I believe Marxist critics such as Lukács) to 'deny himself the methods of hypnosis and even at need the customary empathy',[7] is to require him to deny art itself as a medium of communication. To deprive the artist of magic and empathy is to deprive him of the essential processes of the creative or imaginative activity that have characterized art from Homer and Aeschylus to Brecht himself (who luckily did not always practise what he preached).

Admittedly the ideal of 'becoming independent of the primitive side of his own nature' is one that has been characteristic of many schools of art and many individual artists. It is the classical ideal itself, and the result, in its perfection and severity, is as 'alienated' as any other kind of art. In a very real sense *Phèdre* is as super-real as *King Lear*: what distinguishes such typical representatives of the classical and romantic imagination is not their attitude to reality (much less their attitude to 'the actual world we live in', 'the things of everyday life', etc.) but simply their different conceptions of artistic form. The point is even better illustrated in the visual arts, for even a David and a Delacroix, a Cézanne and a Monet, do not differ in their choice of subject-matter, but only in their different treatment of the same subject-matter. Even a formal classicist such as Paul Valéry in the end admits, as Marcuse notes, 'the inescapable commitment of the poetic language to the negation' (of the real, of the actual). Or, as Marcuse phrases the same thought: 'Creating and moving in a medium which presents the absent, the poetic language is a language of cognition – but a cognition which subverts the positive. In its cognitive function, poetry performs the great task of thought: *le travail qui fait vivre en nous ce qui n'existe pas.*[8]

To return to the actual condition of the arts in our technological civilization, I would suggest in the first place that it is a mistake to generalize their characteristics. Apart from the artificial division between bourgeois 'free' art and a regimented socialist realism (a division that disappears as soon as the restrictions are removed, as in Poland and Jugoslavia) there is no real unity among the various schools of Western art. Surrealism may be stretched as a category to include not only the systematic alienation of the Surrealists proper (the systematic *dérèglement* of the senses, or, to quote from Breton's definition, 'thought's dictation, in the absence of all control exercised by the reason and outside all aesthetic and moral preoccupations'), but also all those distortions of the images of the 'actual world' that characterize expressionistic art of all kinds, from Picasso to Max Beckmann (I would propose the latter as a rough equivalent to Brecht). But outside such a comprehensive category we find, not only various examples of constructivism or neo-plasticism (perhaps the rough equivalents of Paul Valéry's poetry, for theirs too is *le travail qui fait vivre en nous ce qui n' existe pas*) but also, still distinct, those forms of 'action painting' so prevalent in the United States, Japan and

Germany which are realistic in the sense that they project immediate sensations, trace gestures which are not so much symbolic as dynamic, an overflow not of emotions but of energies, muscular exertions that have style only in the sense that a boxer or a bullfighter has style. As for 'pop art' and 'op art', these are significant only as secondary phenomena, as attempts to 'desublimate' art and thus bring it on to the plane of one-dimensional society, pop art by destroying the boundaries between art and the images of mass-communication (ads and comics), op art by destroying the boundaries between art and the scientific 'sign'.

If, nevertheless, the technological ideal is, in spite of all temporary divisions of economic policy and social structure, the attainment of a 'pacified existence', a human society without conflicts or unsatisfied needs, then, as Marcuse seems to indicate, art may well take on a new function and become distorted in the process. One may perhaps see the prototypes of such an art in science-fiction. The scientist, though a slave to reason, is well aware of the power of the imagination. Indeed, in a certain sense of which Marcuse is well aware, imagination is easily confused with invention and the more the imagination abdicates to technological realism, the more ingenious become the inventive faculties. Marcuse speaks of 'the obscene merger of aesthetics and reality', but what is accomplished by technological progress is not so much 'a progressive rationalization and even realization of the imaginary', but rather a perversion of fancy, which Coleridge carefully distinguished from the imagination. Imagination he recognized as an essentially *vital* function of the mind, 'the living power and prime agent of all human perception', whereas fancy is a mode of memory 'emancipated from the order of time and space; while it is blended with, and modified by that empirical phenomenon of the will, which we express by the word CHOICE'. Fancy, like science itself, deals in 'fixities and definites' and there is no limit to its power to convert illusion into reality – the space flight is no sooner a fancy than it becomes a reality. The final paradox would be to accept 'the specific rationality of the irrational'; the comprehended imagination (that is to say, in Coleridge's meaning, the fancy) then becomes, as Marcuse says, redirected, 'a therapeutic force'. Art is then indeed in the service of the revolution, but not in the sense of the phrase invented by the Surrealists; the revolution remains in the sphere of technological rationality. The imagination becomes almost totally atrophied.

The historical alternative, as described by Marcuse, is 'the planned utilization of resources for the satisfaction of vital needs with a minimum of toil, the transformation of leisure into free time, the pacification of the struggle for existence'. I confess that this ideal still leaves me dissatisfied because no vital role is assigned to the imagination, unless such a role, therapeutic in intention, is implied in the pacification of the struggle for existence. But art is not concerned with the struggle for existence in the economic sense of the phrase, but rather with the mystery of existence in the human and metaphysical sense. *This is the fundamental reason why no imaginable society of the future, however free from material need, can ever dispense with art.* Though one can easily equate 'pacification' and art's traditional role of catharsis, catharsis was never envisaged (by Aristotle or anyone else) as merely an aid in 'the struggle for existence'; on the contrary, it was always envisaged as a stoical acceptance of man's tragic destiny. The struggle for 'existence' is within the mind of man; in its highest intensity what art is concerned with is not existence but essence. Technology has so far failed to dissipate the tragic sense of life, and we may suspect that this is one achievement that is beyond its powers. It is art and not science that gives a meaning to life, not merely in the sense of overcoming alienation (from nature, from society, from self), but in the sense of reconciling man to his destiny, which is death. Not merely death in the physical sense, but that form of death which is indifference, spiritual *accidie*. In this sense art is committed to an illusion, and the greatest illusion is the demand for reason and clarity, for a resolution in ontological myth of the paradox of existence. This truth about the role of art in society has been perfectly stated by Lucien Goldmann in *The Hidden God*:

'Man is a contradictory being, a mixture of strength and weakness, greatness and poverty, living in a world which, like himself, is made up of opposites, of antagonistic forces that fight

against one another without hope of truce or victory, of elements
that are complementary but permanently unable to form a whole.
The greatness of tragic man lies in the fact that he sees and
recognizes these opposites and inimical elements in the clear light
of absolute truth, and yet never accepts that this shall be so. For
if he were to accept them, he would destroy the paradox, he
would give up his greatness and make do with his poverty and
wretchedness (*misère*). Fortunately, however, man remains to the
very end both paradoxical and contradictory, "man goes infinitely
beyond man", and he confronts the radical and irredeemable
ambiguity of the world with his own equal and opposite demand
for clarity.'[9]

   In *Soviet Marxism* (London and New York, 1958) Marcuse
acknowledges that when Soviet aesthetics 'attacks the notions of
the "unsurmountable antagonism between essence and existence"
as the theoretical principle of "formalism", it thereby attacks the
principle of art itself'. He admits that in outlawing the transcendental function of art, Soviet aesthetics 'wants art that is not art,
and it gets what it asks for'. Marcuse's nearest approach to a
positive definition of the function of art is to be found in another
book, *Eros and Civilization* (London and New York, 1956) where
after an interesting discussion of Schiller's aesthetics he admits
that Schiller's ideas on this subject 'represent one of the most
advanced positions of thought'. But 'it must be understood that
the liberation from the reality which is here envisaged is not
transcendental, "inner", or merely intellectual freedom (as
Schiller explicitly emphasizes) but freedom *in* the reality. The
reality that "loses its seriousness" is the inhumane reality of want
and need, and it loses its seriousness when wants and needs can
be satisfied without alienated labour' (p. 188) – the same 'historical
alternative', therefore, as that presented in *One-Dimensional Man*.
But Schiller's formulations 'would be irresponsible "aestheticism"
if the realm of play were one of ornament, luxury, holiday, in an
otherwise repressive world. Here the aesthetic function is conceived as a principle governing the entire human existence, and
it can do so only if it becomes "universal". Aesthetic culture
presupposes "a total revolution in the mode of perception and

feeling", and such revolution becomes possible only if civilization has reached the highest physical and intellectual maturity' (pp. 188–9). Under such conditions, again the conditions of the 'historical alternative', 'man will be restored into the "freedom to be what he ought to be". But what "ought to be" is freedom itself: the freedom to play. The mental faculty exercising this freedom is that of the *imagination*.'

So once again we are thrown back on this undefined faculty, the imagination. Schiller's definition of the imagination is akin to Coleridge's and may have inspired it: it is essentially vital and irrational, it dissolves, diffuses, dissipates in order to recreate (? in play), or, where this process is rendered impossible, it struggles to idealize and to unify. Unification – there's the rub! Schiller's notion of unification was formalistic – aesthetic form is sensuous form – constituted by the *order of sensuousness*. The Platonic ideal is implied, for what can the 'order' of sensuousness be but the paradigms of physical harmony. But this is getting a long way from Hegel and Marx and I suspect from Marcuse himself. The final choice is between form (which is neither rational nor irrational, but a 'thing-in-itself') and what the Soviet theorists call 'realism', which again is neither rational nor irrational, but 'the given facts' (and what is a 'fact'?). The 'pacification' which Marcuse sees as the achievement of a technological civilization 'presupposes mastery of Nature'. 'History is the negation of Nature. What is only natural is overcome and recreated by the power of Reason.' Nature is not merely subdued: it is transcended, and the result is (or will be) an epoch of joy and happiness. All this the result of *conscious* mediation (science and technology). Technics becomes 'the organon of the "art of life". The function of Reason then converges with the function of *Art*'. This essential relation 'points up the specific *rationality* of art'.

But is a *rational* art possible, now or in the future? It is at this point that I find Marcuse's answer ambiguous. He affirms, quite correctly, that 'the artistic universe is one of illusion, semblance, *Schein*'. This world of art in the past has represented the dark forces of the unconscious, the resolution of psychic conflicts. Art and Reason have been alternative and even antagonistic methods of confronting Nature. But now 'the formerly antagon-

istic realms merge on technical and political grounds – magic and
science, life and death, joy and misery'.

'The obscene merger of aesthetics and reality refutes the
philosophies which oppose "poetic" imagination to scientific
and empirical Reason. Technological progress is accompanied
by a progressive rationalization and even realization of the
imaginary. The archetypes of horror as well as of joy, of war as
well as of peace, lose their catastrophic character.' A science of
art allied to a science of the psyche *comprehends* the processes of
artistic creation, and 'the comprehended imagination becomes,
redirected, a therapeutic force'.[10]

If this is the inevitable fate of art in a one-dimensional society,
in what sense does art survive? Marcuse predicts a society in which
the imagination is released from all aesthetic control, and it is a
vision of unmitigated horror. In its place he calls for a planned
society that would be 'rational and free to the extent to which
it is organized, sustained, and reproduced by an essentially new
historical Subject'. This new entity (Subject with a capital S)
remains a vague concept, transcending the dialectics of the
situation. But what is the situation? The one-dimensional society
is not a universal society, and has no certain future. 'Underneath
the conservative popular base is the substratum of the outcasts
and outsiders, the exploited and persecuted of other races
and other colours, the unemployed and the unemployable.' The
economic and technical capabilities of the established societies
may be strong enough to contain this threat, but only at a cost
that destroys the liberties of the individual: 'the second period of
barbarism may well be the continued empire of civilization
itself'. With such a gloomy prospect Marcuse closes his study of
'one-dimensional society'. Such a society, offering 'no concepts
which could bridge the gap between the present and the future;
holding no promise and showing no success', remains negative.
The purpose of life remains a mystery.

Art has fallen by the way and is indeed impotent in such a
situation, unless it is to be the instrument that ensures 'the
emergence of a new Subject'. This chiliastic concept, introduced
at the end of *One-Dimensional Man*, remains vague, but I doubt
if Marcuse envisages a Messiah. In *Eros and Civilization* he

remarked that 'the discipline of aesthetics installs the *order of sensuousness* as against the *order of reason*' and this notion (which comes from Schiller), 'aims at a liberation of the senses which, far from destroying civilization, would give it a firmer basis and would greatly enhance its potentialities'. But can the senses be liberated to create their own order in a society that has achieved 'the pacification of the struggle for existence'? Is there not some final contradiction between an irrational art and a rational society, between the paradoxical man who insists on going 'infinitely beyond man' and the technological man who plans 'the utilization of resources for the satisfaction of vital needs with a minimum of toil'? If pacification and sublimation are contradictory processes, what then is the difference between the new Subject and the old Myth?

III

The Limits of Painting

A famous fifth-century Chinese art critic, Hsieh Ho, proposed six criteria for the judgement of paintings, and these six criteria, which summarized the practice of earlier generations of painters, were to remain for many centuries the guiding principles of the art of painting in China. I should like to begin a rather critical examination of the present state of contemporary European painting with a reference to Hsieh's six principles, and I shall then proceed to ask how many of these principles are observed in the practice of modern painters. If we confront the art of our own time with the standards of the oldest and most continuous tradition of painting known to history, we may be able to reach a more objective judgement of our own achievements. (*Plate 3*)

Our first difficulty is to find an adequate translation of the Six Principles. I have compared four or five versions, and since I have no knowledge of the Chinese language, I can only offer the general sense that seems to emerge from a collation of texts that are often obscure even to the Chinese.[1]

The first principle is the one that is most difficult to render into a Western language. It expresses a concept familiar to those who know something about Buddhism or Taoism – the concept of a spiritual energy moving through all things and uniting them in harmony. Cosmic energy might be an adequate phrase, but only on the understanding that it proceeds from a single source and animates all things, inorganic and organic. Spirit resonance is one almost literal translation of the Chinese expression used by Hsieh Ho. It will be seen that this first canon of painting is fundamentally metaphysical.

The second principle if literally translated means the bone method of using the paint brush. None of the Western commentators explains why the word 'bone' is used to qualify a method of painting, but it seems to imply giving a structural strength to the brush-stroke itself. The brush-strokes must in themselves be powerful enough to convey the stream of cosmic energy referred to in the first principle – as the skeleton must be strong enough to sustain the flesh of the body. I suppose there is also a further suggestion of organic functionalism – the brush-strokes must be cursive and co-ordinated, not angular and mechanical.

The third principle suggests that each object has its appropriate form. The artist must seek a correspondence between subject matter and expression which establishes in the spectator's vision the identity of the object painted in all its separateness and concreteness.

The fourth principle states that each object has its appropriate colour. The colours used in a painting must suggest the nature of what is represented.

The fifth principle requires a proper planning of the elements in a composition – the composition must show what is more important and what is less important, what is distant and what is close at hand, and there must be a proper use of empty space. The unity of the parts with the whole is implied – again the Taoist doctrine of total harmony.

The sixth principle is concerned with the peculiarly Chinese doctrine of copying – the notion, which is not quite the same as our notion of tradition, that there is an essence, or vital force, to be passed down from generation to generation. Our Western notion of tradition is more technical: we hand on the techniques and styles of the Masters. The Chinese notion does not exclude these, but it implies that there is an informing spirit to be transmitted which is more important than the form itself.

Of these six principles, four perhaps do not require any discussion: we too have principles of 'facture' or brushwork, of composition and colour, which are similar to the principles laid down by Hsieh Ho. It is true that the modern painter is often indifferent to the brush as such, but he would claim that his new methods, whether they involve the use of a spray-gun or a pierced container of paint, convey a sense of structure – if they do not possess the strength or flexibility of 'bone', they perhaps have a molecular structure more concordant with a scientific age. Even the third principle, which requires the artist to be faithful to the object, is true of modern painting even when the object is a state of mind or a pattern of feeling rather than a concrete object with an independent existence in the phenomenal world. Kandinsky, to mention only one example, was very insistent on making his forms correspond to his feelings – the exact outline of the forms being determined by an 'inner necessity'.

The question of reproducing and copying is one which might also be excluded from our discussion, though anyone who has been in China knows what great importance is still accorded to this principle. To copy masterpieces of painting seems to the Chinese to be as reasonable as to reprint masterpieces of literature. We do not insist on re-writing the works of Shakespeare (though some poets of the eighteenth century made the attempt) so why should we repaint in a new style the themes or subjects that were so perfectly presented by the ancient masters. If a painting *can* be reproduced without a loss of quality (and that is always the requirement) then it is a stupid prejudice to forbid such a procedure. In China the successful faker is recognized as an artist, and his works are bought for what they are: copies faithful to the form and spirit of the originals. The only people who have been distressed by this practice are European scholars, who are given the task of distinguishing the copies from the originals.

We are therefore left with one principle to discuss, the first and most important of Hsieh's Canons of Painting. I do not, of course, exclude the application of the other canons to modern European painting – I am assuming that we too agree that even in 'action painting' the brushwork must be organic, the colours harmonious, the composition planned. That many modern abstract paintings do not conform to these principles is obvious to us all. In so far as modern painting is bad painting – bad in the sense that it is clumsy, incoherent and discordant – it is to be condemned.

Admittedly, apart from painting which is to be condemned for these technical reasons, there is much contemporary painting that is well planned, formally convincing, and harmonious in colour, which nevertheless lacks any element that could be described as spiritual vitality. In addition to the Six Principles of painting the Chinese elaborated what are called the Six Qualities. These are all corollaries of the main principles, and the general sense of them is that *ch'i*, the basic force in question, runs through all the principles and methods of painting – that the brush-stroke cannot be powerful or space conveyed or the ancient masters copied unless this force is present. William Acker, to whom we are indebted for the translation of some of the most important ancient texts on Chinese paintings,[2] once asked a famous calligrapher why he dug his ink-stained fingers so deep into the hairs of his huge brush when he was writing; the calligrapher replied that only thus could he feel the *ch'i* flow down his arm, through the brush and on to the paper. The *ch'i* is a cosmic energy that, as Acker puts it, 'flows about in everchanging streams and eddies, here deep, there shallow, here concentrated, there dispersed'. It infuses all things, for there is no distinction between the animate and the inanimate. Seen in this light the third, fourth and fifth principles involve more than mere visual accuracy; for, as the living forms of nature are the visible manifestations of the working of the *ch'i*, only by representing them faithfully can the artist express his awareness of this cosmic principle in action. (Incidentally, this principle of a cosmic energy infusing all things, animate and inanimate, is also the basis of African art. There is a universal force with four basic manifestations – in man, in things, in place and time, and with three 'modalities', those of image, form and rhythm.[3] But there are also fundamental distinctions between the Chinese and the African cultures that exclude any useful comparison at this point.)

Anyone who has seen a contemporary action-painter *in action* will recognize the scene described by the Chinese calligrapher. There are photographs which show Jackson Pollock 'in action.' One hand grips a brush, the other a can, both arms are spattered with paint and the whole attitude is one of physical immersion in the medium. Pollock himself is on record as saying: 'When I am *in* my painting, I'm not aware of what I am doing. It is only after a sort of "get acquainted" period that I see what I have been about. I have no fears about making changes, destroying the image, etc., because the painting has a life of its own. I try to let it come through. It is only when I lose contact with the painting that the result is a mess. Otherwise there is pure harmony, an easy give and take, and the painting comes out well.'[4]

This statement shows that Pollock's method corresponds exactly with that of the Chinese calligrapher, and I should like at this point to suggest that the distinctive quality of one kind of modern painting – the kind we call abstract expressionism – can be traced to an Oriental source. In Europe it proceeds from Kandinsky – a Russian with Oriental blood in his veins, all his life interested in Oriental art; in America from the West Coast, where modern artists have been very conscious of the arts of the Pacific. Pollock himself was brought up in California and at an early age was reading Eastern philosophy and religion. Mark Tobey, who was born at Seattle on the West Coast, a city where one sees many evidences of Oriental influence, made a profound study of Oriental art during a prolonged stay in Japan. All that is most vital in contemporary American painting – I am thinking of the work of Clyfford Still, Franz Kline, Willem de Kooning, Philip Guston, Sam Francis – has had direct or indirect contact with Oriental art or philosophy.

The other fundamental influence on the development of abstract expressionism has been the doctrine of psycho-analysis – again an influence both direct and indirect. It is not always possible to discover the association that any particular artist may have had with psycho-analysis, but we do know that Pollock, as early as 1944, had been 'particularly impressed with (the European painters') concept of the source of art being in the Unconscious', and in 1939 had undergone some degree of analysis by a Jungian psychiatrist.[5] He remained interested in Jung's concept of the collective unconscious, and some of his symbols have correspondences to certain symbols of transformation illustrated or mentioned by Jung. One must be careful to distinguish between an interest in psycho-analysis that proceeds from the spontaneous activity of painting, and a spontaneous activity inspired by a knowledge of psycho-analysis. In general the paintings of the Surrealists were of the latter type: their ideal was an uncontrolled projection of images from the unconscious, an art entirely automatic. That is not Pollock's method, or the method of action-painters in general. Pollock's paintings are direct, but he was careful to point out that they were purposive. 'The method of painting,' he said, 'is the natural growth out of a need. I want to express my feelings rather than illustrate them. Technique is just a means of arriving at a statement. When I am painting I have a general notion of what I am about. I *can* control the flow of paint; there is no accident, just as there is no beginning and no end.'

A Chinese master would say the same. The point I wish to emphasize is that although Pollock and other American painters contemporary with him were influenced by the Surrealists, particularly by Miró and Masson, they developed beyond the Surrealists. It is not, of course, strictly true to describe Miró and Masson as Surrealists – they too developed beyond, or perhaps never subscribed to, the theory of an automatic art as advocated by André Breton. The development from Surrealism to Abstract Expressionism (in which more general term I include Action Painting) is a development from a doctrinaire and literary conception of the role of the unconscious in art to a painterly and essentially pragmatic reliance on the unconscious. It is essentially a spiritual difference, as I shall now try to explain.

'A painting has a life of its own,' said Pollock. Breton would not have said that, even as a theoretical generalization, and Surrealists such as Max Ernst or Salvador Dali did not conceive their paintings as spontaneous in this sense. Spontaneity, which has also been the ideal of poets such as Walt Whitman and D. H. Lawrence, should be clearly distinguished from the automatism practised by painters such as Max Ernst and Salvador Dali. Indeed, the conditions demanded by Breton for poetry – the uncontrolled projection of images from the unconscious – are inappropriate to painting, which requires between the image and its projection the exercise of a deliberate technique. Automatic poetry could

be achieved by an effort similar to that of a remembered dream,
an exercise which improves with practice. But even in the task of
recording the images present in a dream, which involves the use
of those signs we call *words*, there intervenes a process of intel-
lection. *A method* is involved. The words may be spontaneously
suggested by unconscious associations, but association is already
a selective process, as is again evident from the researches of
psycho-analysis. It was said by a French critic long ago that nothing
is so *determinist* in nature as the association of image with image,
or image with word, that takes place in the projection of dream
imagery. The whole method of psycho-analysis is based on an
experimental demonstration of the causal connection of image
with image in spontaneous association. A single complex lies at
the base of such unexpected collocations. But art is not determined
or determinate in this way. It is, indeed, an immense effort to
achieve freedom of association. To relax the intellectual control
of images is not the way to such freedom; on the contrary, it is
to put the imagination at the mercy of unknown forces, instincts,
or desires. It is perhaps for this reason alone that the Surrealist
movement, which seemed for so long to offer the possibility of a
new art, an art 'in the service of revolution', was finally to break
up, and now, in retrospect, in comparison with the art that has
actually been revolutionary in our time, it seems to have been
essentially academic.[6] I hope I shall not be misunderstood at this
point: I supported the Surrealist movement in the 'thirties and I
would support it again were the circumstances still the same. But
we have learned from experience – our aesthetic no less than our
social experience – and we have moved towards a more revolutionary art precisely because Surrealism as a philosophy of art
was not adequate for a new situation. I believe that it was not
adequate because it did not conform to the first of the Six Canons
of Painting: it lacked spirit resonance, or *ch'i*. It was committed
to a materialistic philosophy, namely Marxism.

It has been a commonplace criticism of Surrealist painting that
it was 'literary'. By this word some critics may have meant to
convey the lack of a vital harmonizing force, explicit in each
brush-stroke. But this is not the real distinction between automatism and spontaneity. Only a consideration of the two painters

who were to have most influence on the emergent American school – André Masson and Joan Miró, can serve to make this distinction clearer. (*Plates 4, 5*)

These two artists in particular have often been denounced as 'literary' – since all thought and feeling in painting, as Georges Limbour once remarked when writing about Masson, is disparagingly called literature. Let us concentrate for the moment on Masson, since he is a highly literate artist, familiar with philosophy and capable of giving a verbal description of his intentions in painting. It is probably for this reason (for the critics and their public distrust a versatile artist) that Masson has never been given the recognition he deserves. For it was Masson who was to be the source of the new vitality that came into the modern movement in the last years of the Second World War.

What has been, what still is, the nature of this vital impulse in Masson? It is nothing other than the spiritual energy, the *ch'i* of the First Canon. Let me demonstrate this by reference to the indications which Masson himself has given on various occasions.

In the *Anatomy of My Universe*, a book of drawings which Curt Valentin published in New York in the year 1943, a date to be noted, Masson quotes Goethe's well-known statement on the significance of visual images:

'We talk too much, we should talk less and draw more. As for me, I should like to renounce the word, and, like plastic nature, speak only in images. This fig-tree, this serpent, this cocoon exposed to the sun before this window, all these are only profound seals; and he who can decipher their true sense, can in the future do without spoken or written language. . . . Look, – he added, pointing to a multitude of plants and fantastic figures which he had just traced on the paper while talking – here are really bizarre images, really mad, and yet they would be twenty times more so if the type did not exist somewhere in nature. In drawing, the soul recounts a part of its essential being and it is precisely the deepest secrets of creation, those which rest basically on drawing and sculpture, that the soul reveals in this way.'

It is precisely the deepest secrets of nature that the soul reveals in the act of drawing – such is the belief of Masson. The artist

creates a universe of graphic forms, forms already plastic like
dreams, and these imagined forms are the product of the artist's
'impassioned meditation'. At the beginning of all things is the
submerged world of unsatisfied instinct, and Masson quotes
Nietzsche, the philosopher whom, as he told Georges Charbonnier,
he had discovered at the age of sixteen and who seemed then to
have fallen from the skies to give him birth, and has remained
always his demiurge. Nietzsche was perhaps the first to observe,
what is now accepted as commonplace, that 'our dreams compensate, in a certain measure, for the starvation of our instincts
during the day'. But the dream, Masson continues, is not content
to compensate for what is cold and abstract in our waking
thought: and to illustrate what he means he relates the following
incident:

'One summer evening, after a day spent in clearing a field,
I had a conversation with a friend on the relative merits of the
philosophies of Heraclitus and Husserl, and the following night
there appeared to me in a dream:

'A bed of grass surrounded on all sides by a brook of very
pure water, but singular in that far from being immobile as it
should be according to the laws of nature, it was, on the contrary,
a rapid stream.

'It was evident that this deep green, but perfectly static rectangle
represented the doctrine of Husserl and that the brook, impetuous
like a river swollen by the melting snows, was a symbol of
Heraclitus who remains for me the essential philosopher.

'All this corresponded to my thoughts of the evening before,
but it was my dream which gave a body to what my reflection
had debated abstractedly the preceding day.'[7]

The rectangle represents reason, the running stream the
irrational. 'I know that I am surrounded by the Irrational,' a
waste-land of infinite desolation, where nevertheless the artist
will realize whatever he imagines. Some time later, 'in the solitude
of the Alps,' Masson 'discovered the flight of the eagle tracing
its perfect geometry in filigrane on the arena of heaven. The
secret world of Analogy, the magic of the Sign, the transcendence
of Number were thus revealed to me.'

The time of solitude in Switzerland must have been a decisive experience for Masson. Georges Limbour refers to it as a time when Masson walked barefoot, forcing himself to be 'hard' in every sense of the word, preferring country paths to city streets. 'He was seeking, beyond knowledge and aesthetic contemplation, a complete communion with the universe. He traversed landscapes which, like that of Montserrat, aroused ecstasy by virtue of their dramatic grandeur, the violence of their forms and colours. But what one calls the ineffable or the unspeakable is the limit where all contemplation ends.' There Masson experienced a mystical delirium, reflected in his most disturbing pictures. He was lacerated, Limbour tells us, on the bars which separated him from the secret of things. But Masson himself has described the vision:

'I buried myself in the darkness of the earth, a seed eager to burst out towards the light of day. I desired to be no more than the essence of movement at the birth of things, in order to be more fully *exterior* . . . I hailed the four elements, I admired the fraternity of the natural kingdom; I inserted the knife, the breast and the shroud in the field of the constellations.

'I saw what one sees no more because one sees it too often: the diamond brilliance of the point of a leaf struck by the sun; the dazzling chrysanthemums of the torrent, amorously coveted by the Sung painter; the tresses of living water observed by Leonardo; the harvester of the field of the sun unfleshed by the light and reduced to a skeleton of crystal in irradiated space.

'I marvelled at the evidence of *correspondence*.'[8]

Masson is describing a state of mind identical with the experience of enlightenment or *satori* that is the aim of the Zen buddhist. When achieved this is a state of emancipation, moral, spiritual and intellectual, in which the mind becomes aware of the is-ness of things – 'when the mind (according to Dr Suzuki) now abiding in its is-ness . . . and thus free from intellectual complexities and moralistic attachments in all its multiplicities, and discovers in it all sorts of values hitherto hidden from sight. Here opens to the artist a world full of wonders and miracles. . . . The artist's world is one of free creation, and this can come only from intuitions directly and immediately arising from the is-ness of things, unhampered by senses and intellect. He (the artist) creates forms and sounds out of formlessness and soundlessness. To this extent, the artist's world coincides with that of Zen.'[9]

I do not wish to insist on any confusing analogies between Zen buddhism and the paintings of Masson or Miró. There may have been no direct contacts; Masson's philosophy of art may be derived from Heraclitus rather than Zen – that would not matter: there is a universal principle in question, and Heraclitus is as much a representative of it as any Zen master. Heidegger, a modern Heraclitus, has read Suzuki and has said: 'This is what I have been trying to say in all my writings.'[10] Masson has read Heidegger and even had discussions with him.[11] But there is no need to document what is so plainly revealed by the art itself, or by Masson's own statements about his own art. Take, as an unconscious description of *satori*, his remarks to Georges Charbonnier on the nature of inspiration.[12] He begins by hesitating to accept this word, preferring a phrase like *l'état de travail*, a working mood. To define this he invokes the Far East. 'In the Far East,' he told Charbonnier, 'a true artist is recognized by this: before beginning to work, he falls silent, concentrating upon himself for a considerable period. This is how he prepares for work. It means that he empties himself to make way for what we might call a supernatural activity, the creation of the work of art.' Masson then defines what happens more exactly. There may have been a preliminary state of excitement, but this is a preparation for the final state of transport (*l'emportement*) in which the mind becomes terribly lucid, and a certain degree of self-control exists. He quotes Redon, an artist, he says, with affinities in the Far East: Redon once said: 'The artist is not inspired: he should inspire the spectator.' Preliminary meditation does not lead to a state of excitement. It is rather a state of composure, in which the mind ignores its immediate environment and penetrates into another world. And that, adds Masson, is a state of the greatest lucidity.

Masson then makes a final reference to the Far East. To induce this state of composure the Oriental artist will spend some time in preparing his tools – carefully grind his ink, lovingly contemplate his brushes. But we are not Orientals, adds Masson; we have other methods. 'When I was young I would slash my canvas with a knife, and what I sacrificed was often better than what I kept. But that only showed that I had need of a state of trance. I believe that any progress I may have made is in mastering this trance, though I am not able to do without it altogether.'[13]

I have perhaps spent too much time with this one artist, André Masson, and in particular I have neglected his friend Miró with whom he has had intimate relations, working side by side with him in the early 'twenties in the rue Blouet. But it was necessary to demonstrate a decisive point of departure in the evolution of modern painting which Masson and Miró represent, and Masson, from a literary or philosophical point of view, has been the more articulate painter. But Miró too, from the beginning, has demonstrated in his painting, and in his mode of life, the same need for a communion with nature, for the cultivation of states of lucidity in which the secret of things becomes manifest in precise symbols. There are, of course, temperamental differences between Masson and Miró, evident in the style and colour of their compositions, but the secrets they reveal are the same. Such statements of his aims as Miró has made all indicate their identity with those of Masson – for example: 'Courage consists in remaining within one's ambience, close to nature, which takes no account of our disasters. Each grain of dust possesses a marvellous soul. But to understand this, it is necessary to rediscover the religious and magic sense of things – that of the primitive peoples.' On the same occasion he also paid his tribute to the Orient – 'les Chinois, ces grands seigneurs de l'esprit'.[14] He, too, has had his mystical communion with nature. At the outbreak of the Second World War, in 1939, he went to Varengeville-sur-Mer, and there, he tells us, he felt a deep desire to escape. 'I closed myself within myself purposely. The night, music and the stars began to play a major role in suggesting my paintings. Music had always appealed to me, and now music in this period began to take the role poetry had played in the early 'twenties, especially Bach and Mozart, when I went back to Majorca upon the fall of France. . . .' At this time, too, he read enormously and was particularly drawn to the Spanish mystics, St John of the Cross and St Theresa.[15]

I do not wish to convey the impression that these two painters are, or ever were, mystagogues. 'I remain strictly on the ground of painting,' Miró has declared. Nevertheless, he has also said that it is essential to surpass '*la chose plastique*' to achieve poetry – 'Poetry, plastically expressed . . . I make no distinction between poetry and painting.' As a critic of painting who is also a poet it is not for me to force such a distinction, and I have no desire to do so. The only distinction we need make is that between poetry and science, but that is not our present affair.

It will be said that Miró is out of the question when our main purpose is to discover the sources of what is still vital and creative in the art of today. It is true that he was not present in person in the United States during the vital years when the new ferment was stirring. But he had many envoys there, his friend Masson and above all two art dealers whose pioneering activities in the United States should not be forgotten by the historians of the modern movement, Pierre Matisse and Curt Valentin. From 1932 onwards Pierre Matisse was busy introducing the works of Miró to the American public. From that year onwards exhibitions of his work were held almost every other year in New York, Chicago, San Francisco and Hollywood. Between 1939 and 1945 (the period of the war) seven exhibitions were held in New York alone, including the important retrospective show at the Museum of Modern Art which ran from November 1941 to January 1942. To accompany this exhibition the Museum published James Johnson Sweeney's monograph on Miró, a book with seventy plates, some in colour, illustrating most of Miró's typical works up to that year.

The sources of the distinctively American movement in modern painting are therefore not a mystery: we still have to ask how the movement became indigenous. The seed had been imported from Europe: the plant that blossomed was American. Or was it? Is it possible that more than the seed, the plant itself, had been transported?

Jackson Pollock himself said that 'the idea of an isolated American painting, so popular in this country during the 'thirties, seems absurd to me just as the idea of creating a purely American mathematics or physics would seem absurd. . . . And in another sense, the problem doesn't exist at all; or, if it did, would solve itself. An American is an American and his painting would naturally be qualified by that fact, whether he wills it or not. But the basic problems of contemporary painting are independent of any country.'[16]

This is all that need be said about the subject. Though there undoubtedly were other painters of an older generation who exercised an influence on the new American painting, such as Hoffmann (an artist born in Germany who did not settle in the United States until 1931), such influences do not affect the evolution we have been tracing, which is neither American, nor French, nor Spanish but universal. Our concern is not art in America or in Europe or in Japan: modern communications, especially those of the printed word and printed image, have blurred all fine distinctions of race and environment. Art is one. It always was one in all its essential characteristics; what we discount today are the accidental characteristics in so far as these are regional rather than personal. I do not say this inevitable development is to be accepted with complacency – it is part of the price we pay for a world-wide technological civilization, but what we lose in variety we gain in unity. One world, one art: the alternative is a reversal of the present course of history.

But what does this new universal art offer by way of compensation? I believe that it can offer the highest values of art, those which we indicate by the word 'universal', meaning thereby what Goethe meant by 'the deepest secrets of creation'. Such an art requires attitudes of contemplation and powers of meditation which most contemporary painters do not possess. Nine-tenths of the art we are asked to accept today is modern only in the sense that it is fashionable, and of the utmost triviality and incompetence. For years such a superficial activity has been tolerated because in a period of transition and experiment one should not be too hasty to condemn the unfamiliar. But we have now reached a terminus at which we need not call a halt, but at which we should become aware of the essential nature of the achievements of the modern movement, and of what is still vital in them. I distrust all such words as 'consolidation' and 'revision' – either they disguise the forces of reaction or express a weariness, a failure of nerve. That is far from the mood in which one should now insist on certain standards of intensity, control and expressiveness. The artists who now most clearly illustrate these qualities – and I have in mind not only American painters such as Clyfford Still, Sam Francis, Rothko and Tobey, but also European painters such as Masson, Miró, Nicholson and Burri – these names are a random choice – all these artists are passionate in feeling but controlled in expression, and present for our enjoyment and illumination forms that combine finite concreteness with infinite resonance. In this respect they satisfy the first and most demanding of Hsieh Ho's Six Canons of Painting, which is the first and most demanding condition of any art that aspires to be of universal significance. 'Then substances, accidents, modes of being are fused and in such a manner that what I say is simple light' – these words of Dante are quoted by Masson in his *Anatomy of My Universe*: they represent the limits of all art that seeks to identify itself with the principle of creation in nature. Maybe for light the modern consciousness would substitute space, but the intention would be the same: to reveal the deepest secrets of creation.

That much of modern painting does not satisfy the basic criteria laid down by a Chinese critic fifteen hundred years ago perhaps does not need further stressing. We easily dismiss painting that is crude in execution, harsh in colour or incoherent in composition, but we just as easily tolerate painting that is lacking in rhythmic vitality, lacking in the clear delineation of an image, lacking in any representational intention. These three deficiencies all proceed from a species of visual solipsism. Much of modern painting suffers from what the philosophers call 'the ego-centric predicament', the predicament of a consciousness that finds itself incapable of relating its private images to an external reality. We might call this general state of impotence a loss of concreteness, and it is not a deprivation that the painter has deliberately sought. He is rather in the position of a sailor who has thrown overboard more and more ballast to save his leaking ship from sinking, and now finds himself in the middle of the ocean with no provisions left. So the painter, having thrown overboard not only every concrete image, but also the cables and anchor which might serve to link him with the solid bedrock of reality, finds himself drifting beyond abstraction, towards metaphysical nothingness. His gestures become more and more feeble and meaningless. He floats on the treacherous element of public hysteria, the vast heaving flood of the mindless and mythless bourgeoisie, and his end is shipwreck.

The modern painter has reached the end of his voyage of discovery, and stares into the unknown, the unnamed. To render back to others that sense of vacuity is not to create a work of art, which everywhere and at all times has depended on the presentation of a concrete image.

But how define the image? There can be no question of returning to the mirror-images of academic art, soiled by sentiment, degraded by familiarity. Nor can there be any question of returning to the regressive dream-images of Surrealism, which merely imprison the painter in the private world of his own complexes. Our images must be at once universal and concrete, as were the images of past myth and legend. We might say that the artist has to create the images of a new mythology, but it must be the mythology of a vision that has explored the physical nature of the universe – what a contemporary philosopher has called 'the qualitative infinity of nature'. This same philosopher (James Feibleman)[17] has suggested that 'the art of full concreteness should replace abstract art', and though he does not give us any idea of the kind of images that would constitute such concreteness, we may agree that 'the fully concrete work of art should combine the individuality of representation with the universality of abstraction in a unity made possible through the exploration of spatial occupancy' – a comprehensive philosophical formula that will mean precisely nothing to the practising artist. But the artist knows what is meant by an image and he should know that his art is effective only to the degree that it presents images that have universal significance. The artist creates his private mythology, but his greatness depends on the degree to which he succeeds in imposing this private mythology on the sceptical minds of the public. Modern art has to fill a vacancy left by three centuries of disillusion, and informality will not suffice. The confusion that now characterizes so much contemporary art – one would rather call it an *occlusion* for it is a blind negation of

the visual image – must be resolved. Art must once more communicate with a receptive people by means of a coherent language
of symbols. I am not suggesting that such symbols must necessarily
have correspondences with perceptual phenomena, with the
so-called world of appearances. But unless they have some
correspondence with the universal harmony of which the
Chinese critic spoke fifteen hundred years ago – unless they body
forth a *form* whether of things known or of things unknown,
they remain meaningless and void.

IV

Style and Expression

(i)

Style is one of the most elusive concepts in the history of culture and it is one that English-speaking art historians have been content to leave ambiguous. The derivation of the word from the Latin *stilus* indicates that originally the connotation was personal: it meant the peculiarities of the marks made by an individual using a *stilus* or pen, and we sometimes revert to this meaning when we speak of style as the *handwriting* of a painter. The famous definition of Buffon, always quoted out of its context, equates style with *the man himself*; and Goethe, in a less well-known but finer definition, affirmed that style, far from being a superficial characteristic of art, belongs to the deepest foundations of cognition, or the inner essence of things. At the opposite extreme we speak of a style of hairdressing, a style of clothing, a boxer's or a skater's style. But always, in these popular usages, we refer to a personal idiosyncrasy, or, at most, an idiosyncrasy copied or adopted by a restricted group of people.

It may be that there is an imperceptible gradation of meaning between such uses of the word and the use of the same word in the classification of distinctive phases of the history of art. It is also possible that a difference of degree constitutes in this case a difference of kind. If we shift from the person to the period, from the individual work of art to the works of a school or of a generation or of a city or a country or a race, do we not lose sight of the original meaning of the word? In what sense is the 'Englishness' of English art, so obvious to the objective eye of a scholar like Dr Nikolaus Pevsner, a style in the sense that we also speak of the Turneresque, meaning a personal characteristic of the style of an individual artist, a style which may indeed be generalized and imitated by other artists.

Nevertheless some styles are less personal than others, and we still call them a style. We speak, for example, of the 'animal style' characteristic of the Scythian hunting people of Eastern Europe and Southern Russia, a style reflected in the art of the Migration period in Central Europe and Gaul. Consisting for the most part of metal harness ornaments, this art is remarkable for its consistent vitality, a vitality in which it is not possible, however, to detect the 'handwriting' of any individual artist. Some other forms of art bordering on industry, for example, the illuminated manuscripts produced during the Middle Ages – such as the Utrecht Psalter (ninth century) or the Bury St Edmunds Bible (early twelfth century) – are so distinct and personal in their style that we can trace the work of one particular artist in manuscripts that are now widely distributed throughout the Christian world. These facts suggest that technique controls style, and that some techniques, such as painting and sculpture, take the personal impress of the artist more easily than others (metalwork or mosaics).

As a matter of fact we have a word to indicate the transition from a personal style to an impersonal style – we then call the result *stylization*. By this word we mean a style that has lost its personal touch, has become generalized and adaptable to a large number of artifacts. The stylized products of the Art Nouveau period are a relatively recent example of this process. It may still be possible to find a personal element in the style of artists such as Toulouse-Lautrec and Aubrey Beardsley. An architect like Charles Rennie Mackintosh had a personal idiom that was then copied or imitated by other architects. But the style that spread throughout Europe in the latter part of the nineteenth century was a fashion, a mannerism, only remotely related to the personal styles of great artists of the past, or period styles such as the Gothic or the Renaissance.

Heinrich Wölfflin, in the Introduction to a fundamental work on this subject,[1] considered the whole history of art as a problem of 'the development of style'. He began with the realization that all the elements of a work of art – form, subject-matter, tonality, motive – fuse into a unity which remains the expression of a certain temperament. But it is also obvious that an individual's temperament is formed, or at least strongly influenced, by his environment. It is not too fanciful to suppose, as Wölfflin did, that the general impression of tranquillity given by Dutch art is directly related to the flat meadows round Antwerp, whereas the vigour and movement and massiveness with which an individual like Rubens handles similar themes is the expression of a temperament that reacts against its environment. The interrelations of individual temperament, physical and social environment, training and opportunity can be (and have been) discussed endlessly, and it is not within the scope of this essay to review or summarize such an immense and complex subject. It is sufficient to defend the anomaly by which the concept of style is held to apply with equal rightness to individuals, periods, and peoples.

(ii)

The attribution of a style to a nation rather than a period or a circumscribed school influenced by a particular environment is one of the fallacies of historicism. Nevertheless, nation-wide prejudices or presuppositions do exist, usually negative in character, and as an example I may mention the attitude of the English as a nation to the style which, for want of a better word, we call expressionism, of which the painter known as Grünewald (Mathias Gothardt Neithardt, the *Mathis der Maler* of Hindemith's opera) is an example from the past and Edward Munch is the typical modern representative.

It is partly a question of manners – of the reticence we practise (or used to !) in our social contacts. To paint pictures that deal with such subjects as sickness, death, puberty, prostitution, melancholia, anxiety, terror, despair – may be simply 'bad taste'. It is not that we prefer to forget or ignore such things – we deal with them in our poetry and fiction, but they are not fit subjects for 'exhibition'. Exhibitionism is one of the deadliest sins in the English code of behaviour. So is any form of exaggeration – as is well known, we make a national virtue of 'under-statement'. Far from being a virtue this has always seemed to the foreigner to be the national vice of hypocrisy, but this is a mistake. Hypocrisy is a conscious or intentional act of simulation or dissimulation. There is nothing conscious or intentional about our reticence; it is an inbred condition of stupidity or (more exactly) stolidity.

That is the basic explanation of our rejection of expressionism. But on this basis is erected, of course, all those cultural prejudices derived from a 'classical' education. Our so-called 'public' (really very private) schools and our two famous universities, in spite of all that has happened to European civilization since 1914, are still indifferent to any aesthetic values other than those derived from the Graeco-Roman tradition. The teaching of art or even of art history has never been recognized as an independent subject qualifying for an academic degree, and what little recognition of the subject has lately been conceded is usually linked to classics or ancient history. That there is such a thing as a Nordic civilization with roots as deep as the Mediterranean civilization has never been acknowledged in our schools and universities.

Expressionism is not essentially modern, nor essentially Nordic. We find it in Hellenistic art, in certain aspects of Medieval art (the Utrecht Psalter, for example) and in Spanish art of the seventeenth century. El Greco might, with qualifications, be called an expressionist. Even England has its expressionists – Rowlandson, for example, and even Turner. Nevertheless, expressionism is alien to the whole classical tradition, with its ideals of serenity and nobility, and where this tradition has predominated, expressionism has been despised, or simply has not existed. (*Plate 6*)

Expressionism must not be confused with realism. Realism is sober, factual, precise; expressionism is frenzied, intense, fantastic. Its purpose is not to present, but to move, to give the observer an emotional shock. The Isenheim Altarpiece was commissioned by a monastery at Isenheim in Alsace belonging to the Order of St Anthony. This monastery, which had at the time as preceptor a Sicilian named Guido Guersi, was virtually a hospital for the sick, and specialized in those suffering from gangrene, epilepsy and syphilis. 'When a sufferer was brought in', Dr Pevsner tells us, 'he was first led to the altar and prayers for miraculous healing were said. It is in the light of these pathetic and repulsive scenes that this Crucifixion must be seen.' Dr Pevsner then describes this painting (it is the central panel of the altarpiece) for the benefit of 'uninitiated readers':

'The Cross is a raw piece knocked together roughly and without care. The body of Christ is big and strong, his head large and heavy. Blood pours down his face from the hideously long thorns of the Crown of Thorns, and his body is a greenish-grey, covered with weals and bruises. Horror could not be painted more ruthlessly. To look long at the figure is almost unbearable, though the sick at Isenheim may well have derived comfort from it. The loin-cloth is as rough as the wood of the Cross, and torn as if lacerated in the tortures or perhaps from the beginning chosen to be of no further value. Grünewald was strangely fond of imperfect, torn, ruined materials. Christ's feet are in a cramp, and the blood has run down them from the nail. His hands are forced by the nails into almost grotesque contortions of the fingers. They are outlined against a black night sky which is hardly set off against the dark brownish-greenish landscape below.'[2]

The full horror of this lacerated corpse must be seen at Colmar for full effect. The only comparable paintings I have seen are those painted by Otto Dix of the 1914–18 war – corpses of dead soldiers decaying on barbed-wire entanglements. (*Plate 8*) Grünewald is not satisfied with a peculiarly vicious crown of thorns: for good effect Christ's body is punctured in many bleeding places by single thorns, as though He had been cast into a thorn bush before being hung on the Cross. There are several other repulsive details, such as the gnarled and swollen feet through which a savage nail has been driven. Even the toe-nails are broken and bleeding. (*Plate 7*)

Another panel illustrates The Temptation of St Anthony. The scene is based on a well-known engraving by Martin Schongauer: the Saint is being beaten up by a gang of loathsome monsters – not the ingenious creatures with which Bosch filled his pictures, but evil aggressive animals. Some of them have a striking resemblance to the monsters of another great expressionist – Walt Disney.

I do not introduce this name disrespectfully, but it is a fact of history and biography as well as of art that extreme savagery or brutality is often accompanied by sickly sentimentality. And here I do risk offending Dr Pevsner, for it seems to me that the head of Christ in the *Resurrection* scene, which he finds 'a vision of majesty and bliss unsurpassed anywhere at any time', is weak and sentimental. One has only to compare it with the head of Christ in Piero della Francesca's *Resurrection* at Borgo San Sepolcro to see the difference between real majesty and its theatrical counterpart. (*Plates 9, 10*)

Dr Pevsner might say that we must not compare incompatible intentions. 'Classic moments are rare in Germany, romantic schools and periods frequent, from Meister Eckhardt about 1300 to the Baroque lyrics and finally to expressionism.' This seems to imply an identification of expressionism and romanticism, which I find difficult to accept; a more obvious correspondence exists between expressionism and nihilism.

Dürer and Goethe may embrace, as Dr Pevsner suggests, the extremes of romanticism and classicism; but I find neither romanticism nor classicism in expressionism, but rather the dialectical extremes of brutality and sentimentality, of harshness and sweetness. I find these same extremes, not only in Grünewald, but also in modern expressionists such as Vincent and Kokoschka.[3] But we cannot ignore such artists: any more than we can ignore, in literature, writers such as Dostoevsky and William Faulkner. We must learn to accept them as truthful witnesses to our spiritual alienation. (*Plate 15*)

That the Anglo-Saxon attitude to expressionism has changed and is still changing outside the schools and universities, among the general public, has been evident for some time and it may be attributed, perhaps, to the triumph of Vincent Van Gogh. Vincent invaded the public consciousness as a tragic legend, aided by the wide diffusion of colour-reproductions of a few of his paintings. These reproductions accustomed the general public to the main characteristics of expressionism – vibrant colours, rhythmically distorted forms, emotional intensity. And what it saw it began to like – in spite of the art critics and the men of taste.

An important qualification must be admitted at this point, for reconciliation, not the acceptance of a condition of alienation, is the final aim of art. Human experiences may be said to exist, for our consideration and enjoyment, only in so far as they are projected from the mind into some material form, and I think we may say that these embodiments of experience survive only in so far as they have the specific characteristics of a work of art. Such characteristics can be either beautiful or vital, and are most effective and most permanent when these two qualities are combined in one work of art. Beauty is an objective characteristic – it can be measured or defined (as proportion, balance, harmony); vitality is a subjective or somatic characteristic, instinctive and intangible, 'life surging itself into utterance at its very well-head', as D. H. Lawrence wrote – a well, he might have added, that penetrates into the unconscious levels of the psyche.

It would seem, therefore, that one of the essential factors in art (beauty) is concrete, universal, typical, measurable and for all these reasons impersonal; and the other factor, vitality, derives its energy, if not also its imagery, from a source (the unconscious) which the psycho-analysts tell us is equally impersonal (the *collective* unconscious). Uniqueness is reduced to the occasion on which these factors are brought together in and projected from the consciousness of an individual. It is the event that is unique: the manner, not the matter. This conclusion is supported by the metaphors used by the artists themselves to describe their creative experiences. Paul Klee's is perhaps the best known – the simile of the tree. The artist is seen as the trunk of the tree, gathering vitality from the soil, from the depths (the unconscious) and transmitting it to the crown of the tree, which is beauty. The same or a similar metaphor has been used by other artists – by Goethe, Novalis, Blake, Coleridge, Rilke and Picasso.

It follows that the artist's function is instrumental. He transmits or manifests what comes to him from the depths of his psyche, and in the process of transmission a transformation takes place. He does not convey a unique experience – rather he conveys a common experience and gives to it a definition and precision that did not previously exist. What he contributes is some degree of personal discipline, of concentration and introspection, which serves to release and at the same time canalize and transform into beautiful objects the energies that flow from an impersonal unconscious. This metaphor serves to correct a prevalent fallacy. Common to all theories of art which emphasize the uniqueness of individual experience is this fallacy underlying expressionism – the belief that the purpose of art is to 'express' a sentiment, a mood, an attitude, a state of mind, an impression of nature. But as Stravinsky once pointed out with reference to his own compositions, expression has never been the purpose of art. If music seems to express something, it is an illusion, and not a reality. Expressiveness is simply an additional element which by habit we (the spectators) impose on a work of art – a descriptive label which we then confuse with the essence of the work of art. This 'essence' is an order, a unity, which we impose on the multiplicity and confusion of our feelings (the sap that flows from the roots) and this order, this unity, is its own justification and is always accompanied by the distinctive aesthetic emotion.

What I have called the expressionist fallacy underlies not only expressionism, but also all those doctrines of communication, of social realism, of populist art, which characterize the political and sociological thought of our time. The artist is not interested in experience as such;he is not interested even in the transmission of feeling *as such*. His aim is to establish order among his perceptions and sensations, and this order is, as it were, a tower of strength, something as permanent and as impersonal as the Pyramids.

'When we suddenly recognize our emotions,' Stravinsky has also said, 'they are already cold, like lava.'

This exposure of the expressionist fallacy need not prevent us from admiring 'that moving objectivity and inner grandeur first introduced into modern art by Vincent Van Gogh',[4] which Munch exemplifies as much as Vincent. I would say that in certain respects Munch is the more coherent, the more monumental artist. His humanism is equally profound, and it embraces tragic subjects of which Vincent was scarcely aware – what Strindberg, in his *Revue Blanche* article of 1896, called 'the rapturous wisdom of conjugal love and the voluptuous folly of sensual love'. Munch was the greater humanist, in the strict

1 *Picasso. Weeping Woman.* 1937

2 *Picasso. Guernica.* 1937

濃松生陰撓結煙
苍翠清白五生隅
座客手止紅磨子
不勸力精細舞沒翠洞
庭作敗專追斑穿斜洞
計尚一地洋人路
半年兴生柳小庄
甲寅悦石溪殘道人石

3 *K'un Ts'an. Mountain Landscape. Ch'ing Dynasty*

4 *Masson*
Le Démon de l'Incertitude
194

5 *Miró. Circus Horse.* 1927

6　*Turner. Death on a Pale Horse.* c.1830

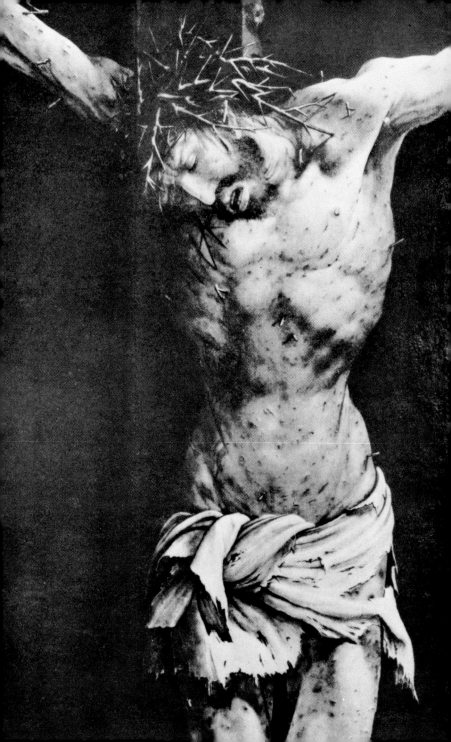

8   *Dix. War.* 1929-32

7   *Grünewald. Crucifixion.* c.1515

9　Grünewald. *Resurrection (detail).*　c.1509-15

10 *Piero della Francesca. Resurrection (detail). c.*1460

11 *Munch.*
White Night. 1901

12 *Munch. The Cry.* 1893

13 *Klee. Angel of Death.* 1940

14　*Kokoschka.*
Self-Portrait with crossed arms.
1923

15　*Kokoschka.*
Mörder Hoffnung der Frauen.
1910

16   Bosch.   The Vagabond

17   *Bosch. Garden of Delights.*
     *Left panel c.*1500

18   *Bosch. Garden of Delights.*
     *Right panel c.*1500

19   *Vermeer. Head of a Young Girl. c.*1665

20   *Vermeer.   Woman in Blue reading a Letter.   c.1662-3*

sense of the word, but there can be no doubt that Vincent is the greater artist in that he exploited the potentialities of the painter's medium to far more purpose – his humanism transcends expressiveness, to create 'spirit resonance', the sense of glory. Comparisons in art are never of much value except in so far as they reveal significant differences. Munch was a humanist in some exclusive sense, and what he excluded was the inhuman – the objective world. His landscapes such as *White Night* (*Plate 11*) and *Summer Night* (1902) are not as intimate as Vincent's or even Kokoschka's; they evoke the mood of the painter rather than any objective reality. I do not know if Munch ever painted a still-life, but I doubt it, for he was not interested in the phenomenal object, the external thingly world. Vincent, however, realized that even an apple or a chair can be invested with glory – like Blake he saw a World in a grain of sand and a Heaven in a wild flower. To point out that the great masters of the Renaissance, Van Eyck or Raphael, also painted no tenant-less landscapes, no concentrated studies of independent objects, does not invalidate this distinction, for in their paintings the landscape and the object are integrated. The separation of the categories that ensued in the seventeenth century was an act of freedom, an extension of visual consciousness, an awareness of discrete existences, and art has been immensely richer since this revolution. But such consciousness can be extensive as well as intensive, and in the greatest art is both. A divided consciousness has its dangers, for it becomes possible to 'specialize', to concentrate on landscape, for example, to the neglect of humanity and vice versa. This tendency inherent in the Romantic Movement was reinforced by the alienation between man and nature that was to be the most disastrous consequence of the Industrial Revolution. It became possible to ignore nature, to confine oneself to the problems of alienated man. To revert to genre painting, or to the *Sittenbild* which is what in effect Munch did, is to ignore the vital extension of human consciousness that had been achieved by the painters of the Romantic Movement.

All this, of course, makes Munch an exponent of the *Zeitgeist*, comparable to Ibsen or Dostoevsky in literature, but we have only to think of Cézanne (or, in literature, Henry James) to realize that a more far-reaching synthesis is possible, some profounder reconciliation of human conflicts. But I have admitted that these comparisons are inexact, and it is a philistine habit to evaluate the varieties of aesthetic experience by some non-aesthetic scale of values, whether social or moral. We may admit with Simone Weil that truth and beauty dwell on the level of the impersonal and the anonymous, but the impersonal and anonymous artist is a myth (a necessary fiction). Let us say, rather, that the artist is one who has a personal vision of human destiny and the technical ability to give effective pictorial expression to it. Effectiveness implies order, unity, but also vitality. The vision, in Munch's case, if not pessimistic, is fatalistic and stoical. Admittedly he was influenced by the yea-saying of that equally fatalistic and stoical philosopher, Nietzsche, but in both cases this was a desperate act of defiance. To get the true measure of Munch's genius we might return to the Icelandic sagas. I have not the knowledge necessary to substantiate this intuition; but from time to time in the history of European culture an infusion of vitality has come from the North – not only vitality but a tragic sense of life infused by this vitality. Worringer calls it the 'uncanny pathos' (*unheimliche Pathos*) of the North. It is the quality that returned to European art, after several centuries of increasing enervation in the pictorial art of our time, through Munch, and no one, not even Vincent, conveyed it so clearly as Munch – except perhaps Kokoschka. (*Plate 12*)

The persistent neglect or underestimation of Kokoschka in England is another reminder of the fact that though nations do not create a style, their acquired prejudices can decisively reject a style. England (and Scotland, not to forget the architect Charles Rennie Mackintosh and the early Scottish Impressionists) was in a very real sense the seed-bed of the modern movement in art. One has only to compare Kokoschka's work with Turner's to realize the close affinities that exist between these two great masters of landscape. But the line of historical development that leads from Turner to Kokoschka is not the same as that which leads from Turner to the French Impressionists; there exist also the devious diversions we call Jugendstil and Expressionism. But the Jugendstil which Kokoschka adopted as a young man (between 1907 and 1912) was a style that had had its origins in England, with William Morris and Aubrey Beardsley, with Walter Crane and the Beggarstaff brothers, a style that had been diffused on the Continent by English art periodicals like the *Studio*. There was, nevertheless, a difference, already discernible in the early drawings of Kokoschka and his contemporary Egon Schiele. This was the new degree of psychological realism introduced into Jugendstil by these young Viennese artists, a realism altogether foreign to Jugenstil itself. The gigantic figures of Vincent Van Gogh and Munch had meanwhile risen above these stylistic trivialities. An early painting by Kokoschka such as the *Still life with pineapple* of 1907 shows the impact of the great Van Gogh exhibition held in Vienna in 1906.

We need not claim a remote English ancestry for certain elements in Kokoschka's style in any spirit of national pride: I am trying rather to find an explanation for Kokoschka's predilection for English life and English landscape, and I realize that it may have nothing to do with art, but rather something to do with our climate, our social habits, our reticence, our fine cloth and good tailors. Such loves are always irrational. And finally it must be admitted that the most characteristic element in Kokoschka's art is not English at all, is even very ungentlemanly, and it is for this reason that, in the past, it has not been well received in English circles.

This element we so confusingly call Expressionism is in fact an exasperated humanism. Kokoschka, as we all know from his writings, is a disciple of the seventeenth-century Czech humanist and pacifist, Jan Amos Comenius. He believes in the possible redemption of mankind through education. He is opposed to tyranny and war, to governments and politicians – I might with justice claim him as a fellow-anarchist. His portraits, which have an equal place in his work with his landscapes, are social comments. Psychologically analytical, they have often reminded us of the curious but not necessarily significant fact that they are contemporary with the psychological researches that Freud was conducting in the same city of Vienna. They (and not the landscapes) were probably the cause of the alienation that for so many years kept Kokoschka from an English public. We have never liked such a deliberate exposure of the man behind the mask. Our portraitists, from Reynolds and Gainsborough to Augustus John, have given a smooth face to the chosen few. It has been part of our so-called social hypocrisy, which is not so much hypocrisy as what we (and the Chinese) call 'face-saving' – the suppression of any demonstration of the emotions as 'ungentlemanly', a form of restraint, therefore, and not intentional deceit. It is this lack of restraint, the bad manners, in expressionism that has hitherto prevented any true appreciation of the style in England, and encouraged a preference for the 'pure' and intimate art of the Paris School – Bonnard, Vuillard, Braque, Utrillo, etc.

Kokoschka is among the few great masters of our time (this was never in doubt anywhere but in England). Admittedly Kokoschka is not 'of our time' in the sense that Picasso and Klee and Mondrian have been of our time. He has never experimented with the traditional concepts of visual representation. He has remained within the world of familiar forms, a devotee of nature and not of the transforming intellect. To quote from a broadcast discussion in which he once took part – 'I always say to my young students: "Never leave nature aside. Don't paint in the studio; in the studio it's poor, it's empty. You need life round you. It is invigorating. You need atmosphere, and that you can get only as long as you are in contact with nature." ' Klee would have said the same, but he would have added that nature must be transformed – transformed to express some spiritual necessity, the *Angst* of a society alienated from nature. There can be no compromise between two such theories of representation, but an artist is not made by his theories, but by his vision. *Das bildnerische Denken* was Klee's phrase; 'the searching eye' would be Kokoschka's. These two procedures now divide the world of art into irreconcilable camps. Kokoschka defends a traditional method of representation, however freely he may use it. He has maintained, against the general trend of art in our time, that the artist cannot forsake the visual world. (*Plates 13–15*)

(iii)

Ruskin conceived the history of art as a gradual progress towards visual truth, but by this emphasis, according to Professor

Gombrich,[5] he 'laid the explosive charge which was to blow the academic edifice sky high'. For the visual truth, once it was accepted as the objective of art, proved to be a very elusive concept for the artist, who thus became involved in a philosophical problem that has never been solved, even with the aid of a modern science of perception. One might say that from the moment Ruskin set up 'truth to nature' as an imperative, art began to diverge more and more from the result that Ruskin and his contemporaries expected, until it arrived at its present stage of total abstraction from nature.

Professor Gombrich's purpose is to show that art never could and never can claim to reproduce 'the image on the retina'. The pattern of that physical stimulus, as recent psychological experiments have proved, allows an infinite number of interpretations, and what we call a *style* in art, whether of the individual artist or of a period, is just one interpretation (or perhaps a family of interpretations) selected from endless possibilities. What remains to be explained, and what Professor Gombrich succeeds brilliantly in explaining, is why at some particular period one kind of interpretation (constituting a style) is favoured rather than another.

His explanation is not original, but it has never been made with such clarity and wealth of pertinent illustration. Briefly it is what might be called the Kantian solution, for Kant argued that 'reason only perceives that which it produces after its own design'. Professor Gombrich suggests that the eye of the artist only perceives that of which it has already formed a design, or, as he calls it, a schema. The artist approaches Nature with 'principles of perception' (to paraphrase Kant) 'according to unvarying laws'. In other words, the artist approaches Nature with a question (what do I see?), and the answer he expects must conform to what he considers reasonable or coherent – what satisfies his visual judgement. In other words, as Professor Gombrich says in one of the many brilliant aphorisms with which his text is scattered, the artist tends to see what he paints rather than to paint what he sees.

It is a process of making and matching. What exists – reality, as we call it – is a mystery that neither philosophy nor art can

fully explain. We probe the mystery with various instruments –
microscopes and telescopes – but also with our capacity for
making approximate charts. The more daring, the more convincing these charts are, the more they express our wonder,
excite our admiration. But what distinguishes a map of the
heavens from a work of art? I am not sure that Professor
Gombrich gives a satisfactory answer to this question. It cannot
be form, for the constellations have form. It must therefore be a
question of feeling, which a map cannot express. If we want to
express our feelings about the heavens, we use the emotive
words in which Kant and Pascal expressed their wonder at the
infinite space above them. Such words represent an individual
and subjective moment of vision, expressed in individual and
subjective signs (tones, colours, outlines, gestures). Whether
words or patterns of colour, the artist's chart gives, as Constable
said so beautifully in a sentence quoted by Professor Gombrich,
'to one brief moment caught from fleeting time a lasting and
sober existence'.

But the problem, as far as the philosopher of art is concerned,
begins there, for what are the qualities that give a moment of
vision its lasting and sober existence? We call them 'style'.
'Human consciousness,' said Henri Focillon in a classic work
(*The Life of Forms in Art*, surprisingly ignored by Professor
Gombrich) 'is in perpetual pursuit of a language and a style. To
assume human consciousness is at once to assume form. Even at
levels far below the zone of definition and clarity, forms, measures,
and relationships exist. The chief characteristic of the mind is to
be constantly describing *itself*. The mind is a design that is in a
state of ceaseless flux, of ceaseless weaving and then unweaving,
and its activity, in this sense, is an artistic activity. Like the artist,
the mind works upon nature. This it does with the premises that
are so carelessly and so copiously offered it by physical life, and
upon these premises the mind never ceases to labour. It seeks to
make them its very own, to give them mind, to give them
form.' Our basic psychological activity is one of integration, of
seeking an equilibrium between the mind or psyche and the
external world. Constable's lasting and sober existence is this
equilibrium, this harmonious moment of integration.

Professor Gombrich is mainly concerned with what one might call the syntax of this language of forms. Why do forms cohere from time to time to constitute *a* style? What is the relation of the forms of art to the forms of nature – or, as he would rather put it, why does the image received by the eye of the artist inevitably gravitate towards a schema that is independent of perception? Although he dedicates his book to a friend (Ernst Kris) who was driven from the study of the history of art to psycho-analysis in a desire to solve such problems, he himself does not rely on unconscious factors. He suggests rather that the mind is like an intricate filing system of forms, and when we attend to some visual experience with the purpose of recording it, we select forms from this filing system and attempt to match them to the unique visual experience. There is no such thing as the innocent eye. The eye is thoroughly corrupted by our knowledge of traditional modes of representation, and all the artist can do is to struggle against the schema and bring it a little nearer to the eye's experience.

Such a theory is obviously true of most of the art with which we are familiar. I find it a little difficult, however, to imagine how art ever began in man's development; or even how it begins in the development of the child. In the case of the child, he begins to scribble and presently matches his scribbles to a memory-image (not to a perception); the form comes before the idea. I have argued (in *Icon and Idea*) that the same happened in the palaeolithic period; man scribbled on the clayey surface of his cave, or saw suggestive shapes in rocks and stones, and with these he associated his memory-image. Again, the form came before the idea. Man or child was not *anticipating* an answer; he had not formulated a question or an hypothesis. His consciousness was incorrupt, his eye innocent. But he was (and is) surrounded by the unknown, and is continually *inventing* or *discovering* a language to describe it. I emphasize these words because Professor Gombrich is a traditionalist and I suspect he would rather emphasize his own word *matching*. It is true that the child and the primitive man 'matches' his scribble with a visual image; but such matching is arbitrary and variable. The scribble, the form, has its own absolute reality, its own individual significance. 'Everything is form, and life itself is form,' said

Balzac (quoted by Focillon). The point I am making is that form does not necessarily need to be 'matched'. Form and its elaboration is a self-subsisting pleasure of the mind – according to Valéry (another French philosopher of art ignored by Professor Gombrich), 'a pleasure which sometimes goes so deep as to make us suppose we have a direct understanding of the object that causes it; a pleasure which arouses the intelligence, defies it, and makes it love its defeat; still more, a pleasure that can stimulate the strange need to produce or reproduce the thing, event, object, or state to which it seems attached, and which then becomes a source of activity *without any definite end*, capable of imposing a discipline, a zeal, a torment on a whole lifetime, and of filling it, sometimes to overflowing.' I do not suppose that Professor Gombrich would contest this observation; but I can imagine that some concession in his theory to the independent life of forms would have made him more sympathetic than he appears to be to the 'manual sorcery' (Focillon's phrase) of certain contemporary modes of non-figurative art.

(iv)

It will be seen that Gombrich, following the example of German writers such as Semper, Riegl, Wölfflin and Worringer, treats style as essentially a 'problem', and by a problem is meant above all a problem of psychology. Form itself is a problem (the title of one of Worringer's books is, literally translated, 'Form-problems of Gothic'). There is no style without form, and though we speak of 'pure form', meaning a form devoid of stylistic idiosyncrasies, it is still possible to regard purity itself as a style (Raphael's style has sometimes been described as 'pure'). Style is always a mode in which form exists. The concepts used by Wölfflin to indicate the development of style in the art of the High Renaissance during the sixteenth and seventeenth centuries all reduce to formal contrasts – linear versus painterly, plane versus recession, closedness versus openness, multiplicity versus unity, absolute versus relative clarity of the subject. These are all *ex post facto* analytical terms. It is not to be supposed that Dürer, for example, deliberately chose a linear style while Rembrandt deliberately chose a painterly style. But it is no less difficult to suppose that these artists merely followed a prevailing fashion. Such academicism (as we call it) prevails in periods of decadence when, for want of an original style, artists resort to the deliberate revival of the style of an earlier period – a process which can excuse if not justify the moralistic attitude of a painter like William Blake, who condemned all painterly styles as the work of the Devil. By contrast this very deliberateness of styles in decadent periods confirms the unconscious roots of style in periods that are originative. In other words, we are brought back to the psychology of the process, which is a psychology of perception.

A psychology of perception should include a psychology of the creative process, a subject altogether too large for this brief treatment of the subject. But it must be affirmed, as against all attempts to categorize style by means of formal analysis, that the work of art, as Paul Klee said, is first of all 'genesis'; 'it is never experienced purely as a result'. Perception is the most vital process in living matter, in man in particular, and it is controlled by instinct rather than by the will. It is multi-directional, arbitrary, and when it comes to rest on a particular object, of which we then become 'conscious', it is already 'forming' a picture out of the amorphous confusion of visual sensations. There is a primordial element of style in each 'good Gestalt', as the psychologists of perception name this primitive act of awareness. The originative artist begins to work at this primitive level, as Klee again will witness – I quote an entry from his diary, written in 1902 at the age of twenty-three:

'To have to begin by what is smallest is as precarious as it is necessary. I will be like a newborn child, knowing nothing about Europe, nothing at all. To be ignorant of poets, wholly without verve, almost primordial. Then I will do something very modest, think of something very, very small, totally formal. My pencil will be able to put it down, without any technique. All that is needed is an auspicious moment; the concise is easily represented. And soon it is done. It was a tiny, but real act, and from the repetition of acts that are small, but my own, eventually a work will come, on which I can build. The nude body is an entirely suitable object. In the academies I have caught it little by little from all sides. But now I will no longer project a shadow of it but rather proceed in such a way that everything essential, even though hidden by optical perspective, appears on the plane. And soon a small, incontestable possession is discovered, *a style is created*.'6

Between the creation of an individual style and the diffusion of a common style throughout a group of artists or the art of a country or a period there takes place a process of diffusion and assimilation. It is not always, perhaps not often, possible to trace the origins of a style to the work of one artist, but there are artists like Giotto, Michelangelo and Poussin whose names can be associated with a style that irradiates from a centre, that centre being a small, incontestable discovery and possession of one individual.

What is the nature of that unique discovery? Is it something that the artist has seen, some hitherto unobserved aspect of nature, or is it an invention, an arrangement of line, form and colour that never existed before? Does the artist within the physiological limits of his reflecting eye, see an eidetic image of the object he has chosen to depict (let us ignore the all-important question of what leads him in the first place to make the choice of a particular subject), or is his version of the object, however seemingly exact, none the less determined by directives he has unconsciously absorbed from his environment?

Gombrich's theory leads to a rejection of any theory of art as an expression of personal feeling – style has lost all its association with the *stilus*, with 'the man himself'. Equally, Gombrich rejects the other extreme which would see style as the expression of some supra-individual spirit, the 'spirit of the age' or 'the spirit of the race'.

The German art historians whom Gombrich criticizes – Riegl, Worringer, Seydlmayr – might object that the conventions that are said to determine what and how the artist paints are concepts of an equally supra-individual and intangible kind. It is necessary in all this discussion of the problem of style to bear in mind T. S. Eliot's distinction between style and individual talent. To identify style with a convention whether of a school, a country or a period, is to give it a body but to deprive it of its life-blood, which always comes from the sensibility of the individual artist. Art would have no history but for the individual artist's determined effort to invent a significant form – a form signifying his unique visual experience. Our basic psychological activity (whether or not we are artists) is one of integration, of seeking an equilibrium between the mind or psyche and the external world. Style represents such a moment of achieved equilibrium. To quote Henri Focillon again: 'Human consciousness is in perpetual pursuit of a language and a style. To assume consciousness is at once to assume form. Even at levels far below the zone of definition and clarity, forms, measures, and relationships exist. The chief characteristic of the mind is to be constantly describing *itself*. The mind is a design that is in a state of ceaseless flux, of ceaseless weaving and then unweaving, and its activity, in this sense, is an artistic activity. Like the artist, the mind works upon nature. This it does with the premises that are so carelessly and so copiously offered it by physical life, and upon these premises the mind never ceases to labour. It seeks to make them its very own, to give them mind, to give them *form*.'[7]

To this quotation I would add another from a critic of literature who has been all too unjustly forgotten, J. Middleton Murry in a book devoted to *The Problem of Style*:

'For the highest style is that wherein the two current meanings of the word blend: it is a combination of the maximum of personality with the maximum of impersonality; on the one hand it is a concentration of peculiar and personal emotion, on the other it is a complete projection of this personal emotion into the created thing. The manifest dangers of talking about style are two: the danger of talking about the accidents and not the essentials; and, in the endeavour to avoid this, the danger of vague generalization. Style is many things; but the more definable these are, the more capable of being pointed at with the finger, the more remote are they from the central meaning hidden in the word: the expression that is inevitable and organic to an individual mode of experience, an expression which, even when this exact relation has been achieved, rises or falls in the scale of absolute perfection according as the mode of experience expressed is more or less significant and universal – more or less completely embraces, is more or less adequate to, the whole of our human universe. In comparison with this meaning of the word Style, others seem to fade away almost into triviality; for this is the style that is the very pinnacle of the pyramid of art, the end that is the greatest of all as Aristotle would say, at once the supreme achievement and the vital principle of all that is enduring in literature, the surpassing virtue that makes for many of us some few dozen lines in Shakespeare the most splendid conquest of the human mind.'[8]

In the end, therefore, the problem of style remains a personal problem, and however ingeniously the historian may weave together the strands that were individual and vital at the time of their temporal existence, his generalized pattern is essentially deceptive. Just as a word like *foliage* is a dead concept unless we remember that it indicates a multiplicity of particular forms, each unique not only as a species among other species, but also as an individual leaf of a particular size and shape, a leaf moreover with vivid colour ceaselessly vibrating in the adventitious winds, absorbing the rays of a common sun and receiving sap from a common soil, so the word *style* is a dead concept unless we remember that it indicates (in so far as it constitutes style) a passionate intention on the part of the artist to represent a moment of vision that is unique. There are, of course, many works of art to which it is impossible to attach an artist's name; nevertheless every work of art is a product of human hands, and is so to the degree these hands worked with an infallible instinct and matched the work, not merely with the work of other artists, some of whom may have been acknowledged as masters, but also with the subtlest apprehension and affirmation of their own nervous sensibility. To that degree these works of art achieved a combination of vitality and beauty we call style. Style is not imitation; style is not the matching of making to any bloodless concept; style, to repeat Goethe's definition once more, 'rests on the deepest foundations of cognition, on the inner essence of things, in so far as this is given to us to comprehend in visible and tangible forms'.

PART TWO

V

Hieronymus Bosch: Symbolic Integration

If, as I have already proposed, we accept the distinction which Coleridge and other philosophers of the Romantic Period made between the imagination and fancy, then in the art of painting there is no better representative of the second faculty than Hieronymus Bosch. He indeed practised 'a mode of memory emancipated from the order of time and space'; he had 'no other counters to play with, but fixities and definites', and 'equally with the ordinary memory' his fancy received all its materials 'ready made from the law of association'. But having made this distinction, it is still necessary to define the manner in which Bosch elaborated his fancy.

Though Bosch lived at the dawn of the Renaissance, he is essentially a late medieval or Gothic artist. He was a religious mystic, not yet touched by any desire to assert his own individuality. Any meaning we may discover in his paintings is transcendental, not humorous or whimsical. The human beings he depicts are not so much 'personalities' as types. We recognize his work, not by its style, but by its exceptional content. He is an image-maker, a symbolist, and our main task, as critics, is to interpret his message.

The traditional approach to the work of Bosch has been to treat him as a 'faizeur de diables', a man who allowed his fancy free and undisciplined range, an artist whose only aim was to amuse us, to shock us, even to terrify us. In reaction to this super-

ficial treatment there have been, in recent years, two methods of
investigation which we might call the psychological and the
iconographical. The first, at its crudest and least aesthetic, seeks
to interpret Bosch's symbols by the techniques of psycho-analysis;
at its most subtle and perceptive, as in the monograph by Charles
de Tolnay, it analyses Bosch's art in order to reveal his spiritual
aspirations. The second or iconographical method of investigation, represented by Wilhelm Fränger, attempts to relate Bosch's
paintings to specific documents and religious beliefs. There seems
to be no reason why both methods should not be combined: if
the images correspond to specific ideas, then we can determine
to what extent Bosch's illustration of them was idiosyncratic.

We may begin by dividing Bosch's work into two categories,
which do not seem to have any chronological significance. There
are, in the first place, the *genre* subjects, typified by the painting
in the Boymans Museum, Rotterdam, usually known as *The
Prodigal Son* (the biblical prototype of alienation) but more
probably representing a *Vagabond* (still a prototype of alienation).
To this category also belong the straightforward representations
of biblical themes, such as *The Crowning with Thorns* in the
National Gallery, London, or *Christ carrying the Cross* in
the Museum at Ghent. This category from a stylistic point of
view might also be called *realistic*, and Bosch is recognized as one
of the pioneers of realism in European painting.

The second category includes all those works which made
Bosch so unique – the highly complex, symbolic compositions
such as *The Hay Wain* and *The Garden of Delights*. The latter
is interpreted by Fränger as a representation of *The Millennium*.

To these two categories of subject-matter correspond two
methods of composition. The realistic-religious paintings follow
the traditional method of grouping the figures within the
picture-space according to some conventional geometrical
scheme – diagonal, pyramid or circle. *The Vagabond* is a good
illustration: the circular space is divided by a diagonal line formed
by the stick he carries, the fore-arm holding the hat, the cobbler's
awl stuck in his hat. The forward motion of the figure is balanced
by his backward glance; the geometrical structure of the brothel
he has just left by the similar structure of the gate he is about to

pass through. There are several other minor correspondences which serve to clinch the over-all unity of the composition and prove that Bosch was a craftsman of supreme intelligence.

The symbolic paintings, however, follow a different method of composition, determined by the complexity of their subject matter. Whatever credence art scholars may finally give to Fränger's interpretation of these compositions (which I shall discuss presently) he has clearly demonstrated that their structure is not arbitrary, that they can be 'read' sequentially, and that their serpentine composition, receding from a detailed foreground to the infinite space of the cosmos, is determined by a precise purpose, 'a perfect simultaneity of vision and thought'. There are other medieval paintings of equal complexity – the many representations of *The Last Judgement*, for example, but these tend to be 'compartmented' (even divided into several separate panels). Even a strictly comparable composition, such as the Van Eyck *Adoration of the Lamb* at Ghent, apart from being split up into ten separate panels, shows, in its central composition, a symmetrical tidiness altogether different from Bosch's complex phantasmagoria.

Bosch, whose proper name was Hieronymus van Aken, was active in the town of 's Hertogenbosch (Bois-le-Duc) between 1480–1516, the period of disintegration and intellectual despair so brilliantly described by Huizinga in *The Waning of the Middle Ages*. But Bosch is in no sense a decadent artist: his style is vigorous, his compositions are monumental, and the message he conveys, however obscure to a later materialistic age, is of great spiritual dignity. His stature was fully recognized in his own lifetime: he was patronized by kings and cardinals. Later Philip the Second of Spain became an enthusiastic admirer of his work and assembled at the Escorial a large collection of Bosch's paintings. Though his influence is obvious on artists such as Patinier, Harri met de Bles, Pieter Huys and Teniers, and may be found in the work of artists so diverse as Altdorfer, Callot, and even El Greco, his style is too idiosyncratic to be easily assimilated. It is difficult to trace the origins of this style. His earliest work (for example, the *Crucifixion* in the Franchomme Collection, Brussels) conforms to the Netherlandist tradition we associate

with the work of Dieric Bouts and Roger van der Weyden, but
his more characteristic paintings, even presumably early works
such as the *Seven Deadly Sins* and *The Cure of Folly* (in the Prado)
seem to derive from some more popular tradition, such as the
woodcuts and prints that had a wide circulation among the masses
during the fifteenth century. Indeed, one may say that although
Bosch's work appealed to the aristocracy of his time, he was
essentially a man of the people, of humble origins and of what
we would now call 'democratic sympathies'. In what is surely
his most moving picture, *The Vagabond*, he seems to identify
himself with the outcast, the alienated 'outsider'. His Christ, in
several pictures, is a sensitive, suffering man, and his saints, above
all the *St John on Patmos* (Staatliche Museum, Berlin) and the
St John the Baptist in the Desert, are men of a sensitive, poetic
nature. (His portrait, a drawing in the library at Arras, shows the
same sensitive, poetic nature: it has a certain similarity to the
portraits of William Blake.)

Bosch is characterized above all by his systematic symbolism –
systematic in the sense that the same symbols, with obviously
identical significance, appear in more than one work. But there
are degrees of complexity in the meaning of these symbols;
and discretion in the use of them. In *The Vagabond*, for example
(*Plate 16*), the symbols are obvious enough. As I have already
said, there is no good reason for identifying this figure with the
Prodigal Son – the same figure is repeated on the exterior of the
wings of the *Hay Wain* triptych and in this representation there
is no brothel or inn, or other signs we would associate with the
Prodigal Son. Moreover, the man depicted is elderly and he is
seen passing through a landscape where various scenes of violence
are taking place, and where various symbols of death (a skull,
several bones, two black crows and a gibbet) are to be seen. In
both versions the man is carrying a basket on his back, which is
a symbol of prudence rather than of prodigality. It is more
reasonable to suppose that the figure represents a pilgrim, making
his progress, like Bunyan's Christian, through a wicked world.
He has a stick and a dagger to protect himself, a spoon to feed
himself with, an awl to repair his shoes. The cat's skin hanging
from his basket is a popular charm against evil (or against rheuma-

tism, as one critic suggests), as is also the pig's foot projecting from the front of his coat. His bandaged leg shows that he has been wounded, perhaps by another cur. Some critics suppose the pilgrim to be a representation of Bosch himself, though the features do not resemble those of the portrait already mentioned.

A little more complex is the symbolism associated with the Saints. *St John the Baptist*, apart from the conventional symbol of the Lamb, has only some fantastic vegetation, the so-called 'fleurs du mal' (flowers of evil) which in this case do not seem to have any very sinister significance. Tolnay sees in this plan a symbol of fleshly joys, and the bursting seed-pods may indicate sexual potency. They may be simply the fruits of the desert (a very benign desert!) upon which the Saint subsisted. St Jerome (Ghent Museum), apart from conventional symbols such as the crucifix he clasps and the friendly lion, is also depicted with fantastic plants springing from the ruins of a pagan temple; an owl, Bosch's favourite symbol of death, is perched on the branch of a dead and fallen tree. A representation of *St Christopher* (Boymans Museum, Rotterdam) is a degree more complicated in that, in addition to conventional symbols such as the fish that hangs from the Saint's staff and the bear being strung up on a gibbet in the background, it introduces one of Bosch's most characteristic fantasies – an immense jug suspended in a tree and used as a habitation. The *St Anthony* in the Prado, one of Bosch's masterpieces, is enlivened by some playful demons, who nevertheless do not disturb the Saint whose concentrated gaze is fixed on immortal visions.

The *St Jerome* who occupies the central panel of the altarpiece in the Doges' Palace, Venice, will serve as a transition to a consideration of one of the major symbolic works. Again we have a symbol of overthrown paganism – the ruins of a throne against which the Saint kneels, again we have fantastic plants and sinister birds and animals. The pagan architecture includes an elaborate column from which an idol is falling; on the column itself the figure of a pagan worshipper. The throne has various engraved scenes which include a representation of Judith and Holofernes and a knight slaying a unicorn; in front of the Saint himself a Crucifix is suspended from the branch of a withered tree.

This painting is the central panel of a triptych, the wings of which show representations of (right) the Temptation of St Anthony and (left) St Egidius. It is on the right wing that Bosch displays a wealth of his characteristic symbols – various fantastic demons and in the background a village and its church on fire.

What I have called the major symbolic works are four in number, *The Hay Wain* formerly in the Escorial, now in the Prado Museum, *The Temptation of St Anthony* in the National Museum of Lisbon, *The Last Judgement* in the Academy of Fine Arts, Vienna, and the *Garden of Delights* triptych also now in the Prado. To analyse these four masterpieces in detail would exceed my present purpose, but it is evident that the same intelligence, using the same symbolic vocabulary, is expressing itself in all these paintings. *The Garden of Delights*, the object of Fränger's analysis, is the most complex of these works, and since it is important to discuss his hypothesis, I will concentrate on this work.

We must begin with some general observations on Bosch's vision of the world, a philosophy which was basically Christian but at the same time critical of the institutions of the Church, above all the monasteries. Bosch undoubtedly belonged to that reformist movement which was presently to be represented by the great figures of Erasmus and Luther. We know that he belonged to the Confraternity of Our Lady, in whose registers his name is recorded from 1480 onwards (his death is recorded in the same registers in 1516). The records also tell us that Bosch supplied designs for a crucifix and windows in the chapel of the Confraternity in the cathedral at 's Hertogenbosch. But the membership of this Confraternity, though a mark of devotion, would not in itself account for Bosch's 'mode of visual thought' nor for the complex symbolism which is displayed in the great triptychs. It has therefore been suggested by Wilhelm Fränger that Bosch belonged to another and more secret organization, the Brothers and Sisters of the Free Spirit, and that his symbolism is a coherent representation of the beliefs of this heretical sect.

Fränger's hypothesis (as it must be called, since there is no documentary evidence to support it) has divided the art historians of the world. Most of them have rejected it, simply on the lack of evidence, and have not bothered to examine the logic of

Fränger's method of interpretation. That magisterial authority, Professor Erwin Panofsky, in his *Early Netherlandish Painting* (Harvard University Press, 1953) says that he is 'profoundly convinced that he (Bosch), a highly regarded citizen of his little home town and for thirty years a member in good standing of the furiously respectable Confraternity of Our Lady (*Lieve-Vrouwe-Broederschap*), could not have belonged to, and worked for, an esoteric club of heretics, believing in a Rasputin-like mixture of sex, mystical illumination and nudism, which was effectively dealt with in a trial in 1411 and of which no one knows whether it ever survived this trial.' Nevertheless, heretical sects within the Church, such as the Bogomils, the Albigenses and the Catharists did survive for many years in spite of, and because of persecution by the orthodox Church, and it is not unreasonable to suppose that a sect so widespread as the Brothers and Sisters of the Free Spirit, sometimes known as the Adamites, did survive the trial and condemnation of one Carmelite friar in the city of Cambrai. A member of this sect or not, it is obvious that Bosch's symbolism is complex and esoteric, and at the same time consistent. Piecemeal explanations of one symbol here and another there, one appealing to astrology, another to psychoanalysis or demonology, are not so convincing as an hypothesis that includes all the symbols in one comprehensive explanation. Even a critic of Fränger such as Professor Baldass, admittedly the leading authority on Bosch, asserts that Bosch's ideas 'constitute a clearly defined programme'. Are we to assume that Bosch worked out this clearly defined programme himself? It seems much more likely that it was the programme of a sect, and Fränger's hypothesis, open to criticism as it certainly is, holds the field until an equally comprehensive and more convincing hypothesis takes its place.

The Brotherhood of the Free Spirit seems to have derived its main doctrine from the twelfth-century Christian mystic, Joachim of Floris, and it is just possible that Bosch was inspired by the same source. Joachim divides the history of humanity into three periods – the age of the Law, or of the Father, the age of the Gospel, or of the Son, and the age of the Spirit, which will bring the ages to an end. Before each of these ages there is a period of incubation, or initiation; the first age begins with Abraham, but the period of initiation with the first man, Adam. The initiation period of the third age begins with St Benedict, while the actual age of the Spirit is not to begin until 1260, the Church – *mulier amicta sole* (Rev. XII, I) – remaining hidden in the wilderness for 1260 days. This conception of history (I take this summary from the eleventh edition of the Encyclopaedia Britannica) is richly elaborated in the voluminous writings of Joachim, and his ideas, never formally condemned by the Church, persisted certainly to the sixteenth century, and were propagated by various orders, the Segarellists, the Dolcimists, and above all by the 'Spirituals', Franciscans who proclaimed the coming of Joachim's third age.

According to Fränger the concept of these three epochs determines the structure of the *Garden of Delights* triptych (which he re-names *The Millennium*). *The Last Judgement* and *The Hay Wain* present alternative interpretations, indeed, as Fränger admits, totally different conceptions of the Garden of Eden, *The Millennium* being an optimistic, the others a pessimistic, version of the value of earthly life.

Fränger's interpretation of the *Garden of Delights* triptych must be read in all its detail – one hundred and fifty pages of close analysis. He succeeds in demonstrating that 'what was previously regarded as only the uncontrolled ravings of a mind that was a prey to the medieval obsession with the Devil . . . now turns out to be a system of sexual-ethical teachings, in which the pictorial motifs were didactic symbols, and above all clear reflections of Renaissance natural philosophy, and hence patterns of a modern intellectual kind, pointing towards the future'. Let us take one example of the method which Fränger uses to substantiate this bold claim – the strange Monster that dominates the Hell of the right wing of the triptych and is probably the most haunting image in all Bosch's work. (*Plates 17, 18*)

Fränger rightly observes that up to the present the significance of this monster has never been explained. 'Like so many of Bosch's unexplained symbols, it has been regarded only as the grotesque product of a demonomanic obsession.' According to Fränger, the monster represents the Tree of Knowledge, 'gaunt and racked, standing in the centre of Hell, a counterpart of the Tree of Life in the centre of the Garden of Eden' (seen in the left wing of the triptych). The Tree of Life is turned into a Tree of Death. The fact that it has no roots in earth, but forms the mast of a ship, indicates that it is 'the uncertain ship of time, the transient vessel drifting in the ocean of the eternal element'. All other details, the scene on the disc which the monster bears on his head (the world-disc), the bagpipe (a symbol of vanity), the procession round the disc, the tavern-scene in the broken egg-shell of a body (tree-male principle, egg-female principle), the monster's backward glance (striving Lucifer-like for knowledge), all are contributory symbols to the one symbolic form, which represents the Ego, the corrupted nature of sensual man.

It is an ordered world of 'signatures', and what Fränger emphasized is that Bosch, in these great masterpieces, has learnt not only to *see* and *know*, but has gained beyond these 'the *vision* and *understanding* that come from a deeper perception, one that combines an infallible eye for the characteristic detail of an object with a feeling for its inner nature'. Tolnay, in his great essay on Bosch, which for the first time established a credible chronological corpus of his work, comes to a conclusion no less positive. This painter, he says, not only reveals the vanity and disquieting beauty of the world as we know it; his revelation leads to a new range of consciousness, no longer entirely linked to religious teachings, but announcing an independence of spirit that will prevail over future generations. Even the cautious Baldass ends by claiming that the outstanding feature of Bosch's achievement as a whole, which is unique in the history of art and has for so long been misunderstood, 'is the coherence and lucidity of his conception of the world, manifest in every painting he produced. Such qualities are only to be found in the true spiritual leaders of humanity'.

It may be objected that an art that remains so esoteric and mysterious cannot justify such sweeping claims. But we have learnt in our time, which was a common assumption in Bosch's time and not subject to a sceptical intelligence, that the power of the symbol is most effective when received uncritically. Bosch's eschatological visions are not part of our enlightened cosmology:

Hell and eternal torment no less than the serene joys of Paradise are therefore no longer significant symbols for modern man. Such is our complacent assumption, but why then are we fascinated by Bosch's paintings? Because, I suggest, they correspond so closely to our dreams. They are not representations of dreams, though we may suppose Bosch derived many of his images from his dreams. As Jung pointed out in his autobiography (*Memories, Dreams, Reflections*, 1963) 'day after day we live far beyond the bounds of our consciousness; without our knowledge, the life of the unconscious is also going on within us. The more the critical reason dominates, the more impoverished life becomes; but the more of the unconscious, and the more of myths we are capable of making conscious, the more of life we integrate.' Bosch is a painter, the supreme of his kind, who by his wealth of symbols, compels us, even to this day, to integrate 'more of life'.

Integration, or individuation as Jung prefers to call it, is first and foremost a process of *differentiation*, the process of forming and specializing the individual nature of a personality. But 'since the individual is not a single, separate being, but by his very existence also presupposes a collective relationship, the process of individuation must clearly lead to a more intensive and universal collective solidarity'. In other words, the individual at the same time that he completes his selfhood, loses his sense of isolation and develops a natural appreciation of the kind of collective life that is necessary for the social solidarity of the group. His personality is no longer either submerged by the unconscious norms of collectivity nor does it react blindly against such norms. The individual is at peace with himself and with his environment.

Bosch may have found such a balanced relationship within such a community as the Brothers and Sisters of the Free Spirit; his rich and complete symbolism is a visual representation of the primal unity and innocence which the members of such a community wished to establish within the limits of their secret society. His *Millennium* is the complex but coherent representation of this ideal of human solidarity and happiness. It celebrates the end of alienation.

VI

The Serene Art of Vermeer

Vermeer is a challenge to the contemporary critic of art and a perfect antidote to that attitude towards life implied by the word alienation. For Vermeer is the extreme example of naturalism in the art of painting – that is to say, of a style that aims to convey, without either the sophistication of means implicit in impressionism, or the selective crudeness or severity that passes for realism, and without any suggestion of the psychological compensations that give force to expressionism, the self-sufficient nature of the motive, of the scene or figure chosen for representation. There is, of course, even in naturalism of this extreme kind, an element of the arbitrary. Every detail in the painting may correspond to a detail in nature (by which we mean, in more philosophical language, the objects or phenomena present to our visual sensation) but the painter has made his choice, not only of a particular object or objects to be painted, but also of the arrangement of these objects in a given space and within an arbitrary frame. Naturalism in art has always been distinguished from photography or the mirror-image by a certain freedom to vary and even to eliminate the constituent elements of a composition. So long as the picture looks natural it is natural.

Naturalism of the perfection attained by Vermeer is due to the combination of two qualities in a painter – vision and skill. By vision we mean, as I have already implied, more than direct visual perception. Vision in art is the capacity to see objects in their essential nature, in their relationship to other objects in the environment, in their substantial integrity. Skill in art is the capacity to effect an exact correspondence between this kind of vision and the image that the painter makes on the canvas by means of his tools and pigments. It is only rarely in the history of art that a moment of vision, in the sense defined, is matched by a perfect skill in rendering the vision. Vermeer is such a rare instance.

I will presently define a little more closely the quality of Vermeer's vision and the process of his skill, but first there are some more general historical circumstances to discuss.

Vermeer was born in 1632 and was admitted to the painters' Guild of St Luke in 1652; he died in 1675. He was, therefore, active as a painter for more than twenty years, and there are various indications (such as the inventory of his possessions at the time of his death) which show that he was a man of substance, living in a good house with his wife and many children (the register of his death mentions eight minors, i.e. children under 23). It is true that he also left considerable debts, and that his widow, who survived him by more than twelve years, had difficulty in settling his estate. But the very circumstances of the proceedings – the appointment as trustee for the estate of Anthony van Leeuwenhoek, a distinguished citizen of Delft and later a member of the British Royal Society, the recorded sales for substantial sums of paintings by Vermeer belonging to the estate – all these facts show that Vermeer was esteemed as a painter during his lifetime. But then for nearly two hundred years he is forgotten. It is true that one or two of his paintings, such as the *View of Delft*, were never lost sight of (this particular painting was acquired by the Dutch government in 1822). Nevertheless, when in 1866 a French critic, Etienne Joseph Théophile Thoré, who generally wrote under the name of William Bürger, became interested in this almost forgotten painter and published an article on his work in the *Gazette des Beaux-Arts*, Vermeer could be described as a 'discovery'. It was only from that year that Vermeer began to enter into public consciousness as the great master that he is. His fame was estab-

21   *Bacon. Study for a Portrait of Van Gogh. No. 3.*   1957

22   *Van Gogh. Portrait of the Artist with severed ear.* 1889

23   *Van Gogh. Self-Portrait.* 1886

24 *Van Gogh.*
Bedroom at Arles.
1888

25 *Van Gogh.*
Road with Cypresses.
1890

26 *Matisse. Decorative Figure.* 1908

27 *Michelangelo. Slave*

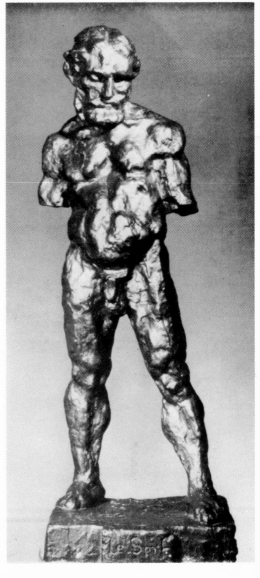

28 *Matisse. Slave.* 1900-3

29   *Matisse. La Serpentine.* 1909

lished along with that of the Impressionists, and thus, in a very
real sense, Vermeer is a 'modern' artist.

It might be asked whether this is merely a coincidence, or
whether there are qualities in Vermeer's work that appeal to the
modern sensibility, and whether these are the same qualities that
led to the previous neglect of his work. Vermeer is not, of course,
the only artist to be rediscovered or re-valued in modern times.
A similar case is Piero della Francesca, and although Piero was
never neglected to the same extent as Vermeer, the qualities in
his work that appeal to the modern sensibility are similar. Let
us now try to isolate these qualities in Vermeer's painting.

I would suggest that possibly there are three such qualities, and
that these are precisely the qualities that combine to make
Vermeer unique. They relate to (1) *design*, (2) *colour*, and (3) a
spiritual or metaphysical quality which for the moment we might
call *serenity*.

By design we mean something more than the arrangement or
composition of a painting. Subjects are selected and composed as
single figures or as groups, as figures in a landscape or as the varied
features of a landscape. But to *design* a painting means much more
than this – it means in the first place to situate the subject within
a credible space, and to give the various elements in the composition a stable structure, a configuration that allows the spectator's
vision to rest meditatively on the scene or subject presented. At
its simplest (but by no means its easiest) this effect is obtained by
light alone – by so modulating the play of light or shade on an
isolated form that it occupies an imaginary space without support
from other objects in the same visual field. The best example in
Vermeer's work is the *Head of a Young Girl* in the Mauritshuis.
(*Plate 19*) In spite of the fact that it was probably restored soon
after it was bought for about 4*s* 6*d* at an auction in The Hague in
1882, it still preserves Vermeer's characteristic modelling, that is
to say, his supremely subtle modulation of light and shade.
Where necessary, as in the highlights of the turban, the paint can
be impasted to produce a highlight, but the features of the girl
are rendered with a soft translucency which seems to proceed
from within the flesh, rather than to strike it from without. The
effect is comparable to the finest tin glazes on earthenware, a

characteristic which supports the supposition that at some early stage in his career Vermeer may have been engaged in the painting of the earthenware tiles and dishes for which his native city of Delft was so famous during his lifetime. This may seem to be comparing great things with small ones, but not to anyone who has any knowledge of the exquisite quality of the best Delft ware.

A contrast is provided by the *Maidservant pouring Milk*, which like the *Head of a Young Girl* can be traced back to the Amsterdam Auction of 1696 and is perhaps a slightly earlier painting (it was praised by Reynolds in his *Journey to Flanders and Holland*, 1781). Here the general effect is coarser, not only as befits an older and humbler woman, but to harmonize the texture of the flesh with those of her bodice and apron, the rough earthenware and the crusty brown bread. But the modulations in this painting are just as subtle as those in the *Head of a Young Girl*, and the chromatic scale is richer, more deeply saturated. The design is much more complex. Instead of a single motive against a uniform background, Vermeer gives us a solid almost full-length figure standing in the light streaming from a window on the right against a clear but gently graded background, which has the effect of silhouetting the long line of the maidservant's back (an 'edge', however, that is not hard, but beautifully fused into the enamel-like surface of the paint – again an effect that is reminiscent of painted earthenware). To correct the isolation of such a solid figure in the given space, Vermeer has placed the laden table diagonally with the woman's pelvis, and balanced this powerful movement, which extends only to the middle of the given space, by another crossing diagonal movement which extends from the basket and brass utensil hanging high in the left corner of the picture to the footwarmer in the right corner.

A comparison of this painting with the *Woman in Blue reading a Letter* will take us a little further into the secrets of Vermeer's design. Here again we have a standing figure occupying the middle space, and since the subject is more 'refined', the textiles (the beautifully painted coat of light blue silk, the woollen skirt, the rug on the table) are rendered more smoothly and with subtle gradations of light and shade. The daylight seeps in from an invisible window to the left, but this time the subject's features are not isolated against the grey wall, but placed against the intricate background of a large map hanging on the wall (an object which appears in two or three of Vermeer's paintings). This allows Vermeer to achieve a harmonious contrast between the lively texture of the brunette's complexion and the background of 'dead' parchment. What, however, distinguishes this picture from those preceding it, and links it with Vermeer's most sophisticated masterpieces, is the geometricization of the design. The horizontal rectangle of the map divides the vertical rectangle of the canvas harmoniously; the rectangular chairback to the left echoes the edge of the map, while the long edge of the chairback to the right balances the shorter verticals to the left. (*Plate 20*)

That this 'geometricization' of the picture-space is deliberate is evident from several other paintings by Vermeer, notably the *Soldier and Laughing Girl* in the Frick Collection, New York, the *Lady reading a Letter at an Open Window*, *The Music Lesson* at Buckingham Palace, *The Concert* at the Isabella Stewart Gardner Museum, Boston, *A Painter in his Studio*, *The Love Letter*, the *Lady seated at the Virginals*, and more obviously but most effectively in the famous *Street in Delft*, which is a complex design of rectangles and rectilinear motives 'developed' from the small bricks and window-frames to the larger windows, doorways and façades of the houses.

Geometry in painting is of no interest unless it serves an aesthetic purpose (as it does most exclusively in a modern Dutch painter such as Piet Mondrian). Straight lines in a painting can have the following functions: they divide the rectangular surface of the canvas into harmoniously proportionate areas; they give clear differentiation to determined areas of colour; and they build an architecture into the occupied space of the picture. This latter purpose is obvious enough when the subject is architectural, as in the *Street in Delft*; but the same purpose is served in artificially posed figure compositions such as those of *A Painter in his Studio* and *The Love Letter*. In both these paintings a very complex geometrical structure sustains the drama in a theatrical framework: a stage is built upon which the figures can perform with dramatic credibility. It is not merely a question, as in all naturalistic painting, of creating a spatial illusion (that, after all, is done effectively in the 'prop-less' *Head of a Young Girl*: it must be an inhabited space – a pragmatic space rather than an ideal one. Of such spatial realism Vermeer remains one of the supreme masters.

Vermeer is also one of the supreme masters of colour harmony. The choice of a particular gamut of colours is no doubt determined by the unique sensibility of the painter: a personal preference in colours is as arbitrary as a personal taste in food or wines. But the harmonization of the preferred colours, their disposition in proportioned areas within the picture-space, their degree of saturation, their modulated tones – all these subtleties of application are achieved by skill, skill in the preparation or mixing of colours and in the manipulation of brushes. Vermeer's colour-harmony is sometimes described as 'cool', and there are certain combinations of lemon yellow, pale blue and pearl grey (as in the *Head of a Young Girl* or the figure of Clio in the *Painter in his Studio*) just as there are certain phrases in the music of Mozart or Debussy, which are uniquely characteristic in the man Vermeer. But Vermeer was also master of richer and more solemn harmonies, as in the *Maidservant pouring Milk*, *The Music Lesson*, *The Love Letter*, and, above all, in the two views of Delft. The large *View of Delft* has evoked many critical and poetic tributes and it is probably the best-loved landscape in the western world. Its beauty may partly be explained by the subtle combination of three contrasted textures – the horizontal sheen of the water, the grained texture of the boats and the buildings in the middle distance, and the infinitely soft gradations of the clouds above. Only Vermeer is master of such a chromatic scale, so resonant and yet so stilled.

Every painting of Vermeer's is bathed in this particular kind of serenity, and this is the intangible element in his work to which I have already referred. There is no violence in his work, of thought or action. There is an eternal stillness, of music that dies on the echo, of the mind entranced by a message of love, of fingers that gently guide a thread of lace, of a tiny pearl suspended in delicate scales. Even Clio's eyes are downcast, as if embarrassed by the symbols of Fame which she is compelled to hold.

We know little or nothing of Vermeer's personality, and it is dangerous to generalize from the evidence of his paintings. He left behind him a large family and many debts, and his life may have been sordid. But a mind that is troubled may seek a peaceful refuge in art. Vermeer is almost as much a mystery as Shakespeare but he is perhaps nearer to another English poet, his contemporary Thomas Traherne (1637–74) whose work was also lost for centuries and then recovered. Traherne was possessed by the same 'Pure and Virgin Apprehensions', in which 'all things abided Eternally as they were in their proper places. Eternity was manifest in the Light of the Day, and some thing infinite behind every thing appeared: which talked with my Expectation and moved my Desire. The City seemed to stand in Eden, or to be built in Heaven. The Streets were mine, the Temple was mine, the People were mine, their Clothes and Gold and Silver were mine, as much as their sparkling Eyes, fair Skins and ruddy faces. The Skies were mine, and so were the Sun and Moon and Stars, and all the World was mine, and I the only Spectator and Enjoyer of it.' This is the vision of an innocent eye, and though there is one painting possibly by Vermeer that is concerned with what Traherne called 'the Dirty Devices of this World' (the *Courtesan* in the State Picture Gallery, Dresden) we are confident that he too lived to unlearn these devices, and to see the beauty of the world in a clear and familiar light.

VII

Vincent Van Gogh: A Study in Alienation

Roger Fry once expressed the opinion that Vincent was 'a more remarkable man than he was an artist'.[1] In this essay I intend to concentrate on the man, but I would like to make quite clear, at the beginning, that I do not share Fry's opinion. It is doubtful if it is ever possible to separate a man and his art, and if one concludes, as Fry did, that 'Van Gogh ends, as one might guess from his temperament that he must end, as an inspired illustrator', then one is condemning the man no less than the artist. Fry's failure to appreciate the significance of Vincent was a consequence of his failure to appreciate the significance of that style of art we call expressionism, of which Vincent remains one of the most typical representatives.

If the style, in this case as in all others, is the expression of the man himself, then it follows that we can define the style by describing the man. Such is my intention, but again I must begin with a disclaimer. To describe is not to analyse: this will not be an essay in psycho-analysis. That Vincent suffered from some form of psychopathy is perhaps obvious, but psychopathy is a scientific term that implies no more than a mental strain or occasional disequilibrium such as most people sustain. It does not mean a psychosis or persistent mental derangement, but rather that sense of isolation and rejection we call alienation.

Professor Kraus, who published an elaborate analysis of Vincent's illness in a Dutch scientific periodical in 1941,[2] refused to give it a specific name. He dismissed as an absurdity the diagnosis of epilepsy, and said that 'there is little sense in postulating a combination of epilepsy and schizophrenia, which some consider probable in the Vincent Van Gogh "case"'. 'As far as I can see,' concludes the Professor, 'one comes nearest to a diagnosis of his morbid condition with the vague description: psychogenic attacks on a psychopathic basis.' But this and all other medical diagnoses seemed to the wise Doctor Kraus to be 'too narrow for the astonishing psychopathic condition of Vincent's exceptional personality – in his art no less than in his "illness" he was an individualist'.

Such is the point of view I shall adopt in a very simple and direct review of Vincent's life and work.

Vincent is unique among great artists in that we may follow his development stage by stage, almost day by day, in the letters he wrote to his brother Theo from 1872 to the time of his death in 1890 – the most revealing account of an artist's innermost self that is to be found in any language.

Vincent was born on 30 March 1853, at Zundert, a small village in the Brabant province of Holland, where his father Theodorus Van Gogh was the pastor. Three of the brothers of Theodorus had become art dealers, and one of these uncles of Vincent, also named Vincent, who eventually became a director of the Goupil Gallery in Paris, had a significant influence on the course of the painter's life. But the greatest influence in his early years was that of Vincent's mother, a woman of great strength of character.

Vincent, though physically robust, was self-willed and aggressive as a child, qualities which did not improve at the village school he first attended. Five more children were born to the pastor and his wife, so eventually their education was entrusted to a governess. In a memoir written by Vincent's sister-in-law, Mrs Van Gogh-Bonger, which introduced the first edition of his letters, we are told that the childhood of these children was full of the poetry of the Brabant country life – 'they grew up among the cornfields, the heath and the pine forests, in that peculiar sphere of a village parsonage, the charm of which remained with them all their lives'. Many passages in Vincent's letters testify to the enduring effect of this idyllic childhood.

At the age of sixteen, in 1869, Vincent was apprenticed to The Hague branch of the firm of Goupil, with the intention of becoming an art dealer. He stayed there until 1873 when he was transferred to the firm's branch in London and seems for a while to have been very happy there. For the first time in his life he fell in love but, alas, was rejected. He then became very despondent and as a distraction began to draw. But nothing availed, he grew more and more depressed and more and more solitary in his habits. He walked about London, observing the English way of living and the English people – 'try to walk as much as you can', he wrote to Theo, 'and keep your love for nature, for that is the true way to understand art.'

His taste in art was already defined. He loved above all the work of Millet – '"The Angelus", that's the thing, that is beauty, that is poetry' (letter of January 1874). He read much – Michelet, Renan, George Eliot, the Gospels. But the depression continued and as a remedy he was sent to the firm's branch in Paris, where he arrived in May 1875. But all in vain; by January of the next year he was asked to resign. In April he returned to England and for the rest of the year found employment as a schoolmaster. But this experiment also failed and at the end of the year he returned to Holland with a deepening sense of a religious vocation. He went to Amsterdam with the idea of taking a university degree in theology, but discovered he had no aptitude for regular study. He then decided to become an evangelist in Belgium, for which no academic qualifications were necessary, but once again he was a failure. A teacher with whom he shared lodgings at this time, P. C. Görlitz, describes him as 'a man totally different from the usual children of man. His face was ugly, his mouth more or less awry, moreover his face was densely covered with freckles, and he had hair of a reddish hue. As I said, his face was ugly, but as soon as he spoke about religion or about art, and then became excited, which was sure to happen very soon, his eyes would sparkle, and his features would make a deep impression on me; it wasn't his own face any longer: it had become beautiful.'³

He had found a job as a bookkeeper, but 'when he came back from his office at nine o'clock in the evening, he would immediately light a little wooden pipe; he would take down a big Bible, and sit down to read assiduously, to copy texts and to learn them by heart; he would also write all kinds of religious compositions.' He would read his Bible, or Spurgeon's sermons, long after he had gone to bed and Görlitz would find him early in the morning 'lying on his bed with his beloved book on his pillow, and then I would wake him up so that he might go where his humdrum little job as a bookkeeper called him'. (*Plate 21*)

Vincent was now twenty-five, and had become what we now call an 'outsider', eccentric in manner and dress, nervous, dejected. It was then that he went to the Borinage, the industrial district of Belgium, to work among the poor, teaching and preaching. But then religious doubts began to assail him; he lost his faith in God and wandered about without work, without friends, and often without food. This is a period (July 1880) of profound spiritual crisis, during which in moving letters to his brother he reveals his inmost soul. 'Involuntarily, I have become more or less a kind of impossible and suspect person in the family, someone who is not trusted . . . the best thing I can do is to go away and keep at a convenient distance, so that I may cease to exist for you all . . . the only thing to do is to hide myself . . . I am a man of passions, capable of and subject to doing more or less foolish things, of which I happen to repent, more or less, afterwards.' And then he utters that pathetic cry: 'When I was in other surroundings, in the surroundings of pictures and works of art, you know how I had a violent passion for them, reaching the highest pitch of enthusiasm. And I am not sorry about it, for even now, *far from that land, I am often homesick for the land of pictures.*' (*Letters* I, 133.)

And so Vincent came to terms with his destiny, in a moment of suffering and despair. 'I felt my energy revive, and I said to myself, I will take up my pencil again, which I have forsaken in my great discouragement, I will go on with my drawing. From that moment everything has seemed transformed for me . . .' (I, 136.)

He was still in the Borinage, and began to draw the miners among whom he lived. And he copied his beloved Millet, obsessively. Millet's *Sower* became a symbol of his deepest convictions – 'I feel so strongly that it is with people as with corn – if you are not sown in the earth to take root there, it does not matter, because you will be ground for bread.' It was his latest as well as his earliest theme – he painted two oils of this same subject in the last year of his life.

Vincent acquired a manual of painting technique, studied anatomy and drew from nature and the living model. Everywhere around him in the Borinage he found subjects sympathetic to his new mood– brown earth and smoky skies, miners with tired and miserable faces, blackened by coal dust, the villages of the weavers. The miners and the weavers formed a race apart and he felt a great affinity for these simple artisans. 'The man from the depths of the abyss, *de profundis* – that is the miner; the other, with his dreamy air, somewhat absent-minded, almost a somnambulist – that is the weaver. I have been living among them for two years and have learned a little of their unique character, at least, that of the miners especially. And increasingly I find something touching and almost sad in these poor obscure labourers, of the lowest order, so to say, and the most despised, who are generally represented as a race of criminals and thieves by a perhaps vivid but very false and unjust imagination.' (I, 136; 24 September 1880.)

By October of this year Vincent, who was now twenty-seven, had had enough of this depressing atmosphere and went to Brussels, where he could study the art of the past and seek the sympathetic understanding of other artists. Theo put him in touch with a Dutch painter called Anthon van Rappard, with whom for a time he established an uneasy but profitable friendship which lasted for the next five years. His letters to van Rappard have survived and are of great interest in that they are what Vincent calls 'practical talk'; they occupy more than a hundred pages in the *Complete Letters*.

The expense of living in Brussels proved too high for Vincent, so in April 1881, he decided to return to his parents, now living in Etten. There he recuperated, read the novels of Charlotte Brontë and Balzac, and fell passionately in love with a cousin, a young widow from Amsterdam who came to stay with his parents. Alas, once again his love was not returned and once again he fell into despair. He became irritable and nervous, quarrelled with his father, and in December left suddenly for The Hague, where he was to spend the next two years. Here he took pity on a deserted woman with children, who dragged him down to her own miserable level. But he worked hard, and the numerous letters to Theo from The Hague, often illustrated by little pen sketches, trace step by step his rapid development during this period. This was partly due to the influence of a cousin, the Dutch Impressionist painter Anton Mauve who lived there and gave him lessons in oil painting. But Vincent was not really teachable and soon quarrelled with Mauve and all the other painters he became acquainted with in The Hague. He resolved to work out his own salvation and was rewarded when in March 1882 his uncle Cornelius, who was an art dealer in Amsterdam, visited him and was so impressed by his progress that he commissioned him to draw twelve landscapes of The Hague. These were successful and further commissions followed.

By August 1883 Vincent had come to the conclusion that he could no longer live with 'the woman', though he was full of pity for her and was devoted to her little boy. He finally broke off the attachment, provided for her as well as his circumstances permitted, and without any undue regret on her part (though with some remorse on his) left The Hague and went to Hooge- veen in the province of Drenthe in North Holland, which had been recommended to him by Van Rappard as being both cheap and 'original'. But Drenthe, too, was a disappointment and he stayed there for only two months. At first he was exhilarated by a country 'where progress had got no farther than stage coach and barge, where everything is more virgin than I have seen in any other place' (II, 337), but finally the desolation of the landscape ate into his heart and he was haunted by the fate of the woman and her two children whom he had abandoned. He described his condition in a series of melancholy but moving letters to Theo. 'There is a saying of Gustave Doré,' he wrote (II, 336), 'which I have always admired: "j'ai la patience d'un boeuf." I find a certain goodness in it, a certain resolute honesty, in short, that saying has a deep meaning, it is the word of a real artist . . . "J'ai la patience," how quiet it sounds, how dignified.' It is foolish to speak of 'natural gifts' he explained, – one ought to have patience, to learn patience from nature, learn patience from seeing the corn slowly ripen, seeing things grow. How can one think oneself so absolutely dead as to imagine one would not grow any more? 'But in order to grow, one must be rooted in the earth.'

But Vincent did not take root in Drenthe. He felt more and more 'that peculiar torture, loneliness' – loneliness, not solitude, and by the end of the year he could stand it no longer. Once more he fled to the bosom of his family, with whom he was now reconciled, and who were now living in Neunen, a village near Eindhoven. He stayed there for two years, painting the Brabant landscape and the peasants, and one or two self-portraits. 'It is a fine thing to be right in the snow in the winter, right in the yellow leaves in autumn, in summer right in the ripe corn, in spring right in the grass, always with the peasant girls and reapers, in summer under the open skies, in winter near the open fire place, and to know it has always been so and always will be.' This is the period of *The Potato-Eaters*, his first great painting. Its quality is indicated in a letter to Theo of the same time (II, 425) about a related work – 'You will receive a big still-life of potatoes, in which I tried to get *corps*, I mean, to express the material in such a way that they become heavy, solid lumps, *which would hurt you if they were thrown at you*.' Such is the new feeling of *Sachlichkeit* in his work.

The two years at Neunen, though full of personal and domestic difficulties, were very important in his development as a painter. He now felt confident in his use of the oil medium, and his style became correspondingly more plastic (*malerisch*). *The Potato-Eaters* is not only, as he called it, 'from the heart of peasant life': it is the crystallization of five years' passionate struggle with his chosen medium of expression. But this painting is an end rather than a beginning, and a visit to Amsterdam in October 1885 convinced him that the secret of the great masters still eluded him. 'What struck me most on seeing again the old Dutch pictures,' he wrote to Theo (II, 427), 'is that most of them were *painted quickly*, that these great masters such as a Frans Hals, a Rembrandt, a Ruysdael and so many others – dashed off a thing from the first stroke and did not retouch it so very much . . . if it was right, *they left it as it was.*' And the colour, too, was a revelation. One picture alone (by Hals and Codde), 'about twenty officers full length', that one picture was worth the trip to Amsterdam. And he then describes the figure of the flag-bearer – a figure in grey, but such grey! 'In that grey he brings blue and orange – and some white; the waistcoat has satin bows of a divine soft blue, sash and flag orange – a white collar.

'Orange, blanje (blanc), blue, as the national colours were then – orange and blue, side by side, that most splendid colour scheme against a background of a grey, cleverly united just by mixing those two, let me call them poles of electricity (speaking of colours though) so that they annihilate each other against that grey and white. Further we find in that picture – other orange scales against other blue, further, the most beautiful blacks against the most beautiful whites; the heads, about twenty of them, sparkling with life and spirit, and a technique! a colour! the figures of all those people superb and full size.

'But that orange, blanc, blue fellow in the left corner . . . I seldom saw a more divinely beautiful figure. It is unique.

'Delacroix would have raved about it – absolutely raved. I was literally rooted to the spot.'

I have given what is perhaps a disproportionately large amount of space to this visit to Amsterdam because I believe that in so far as Vincent is to be classified as an Impressionist, his Impressionism was born at that moment, and was a personal discovery, owing nothing to those French Impressionists, such as Pissarro and Seurat, with whom he was later to be associated. This does not mean that he was in no way influenced by these painters, when, in March 1886, he first saw them in Theo's gallery in Paris; but in so far as a conversion was necessary, the ground for it had been prepared by the revelation in Amsterdam. Before going to Paris, Vincent spent a few months in Antwerp. There he took lessons in painting at the Academy, but more important for the future was his discovery of Japanese prints, of whose existence he had learned by reading the de Goncourts, who had also made him aware of Chardin. He began to see Japonaiserie everywhere, even in the docks of Antwerp. 'One of de Goncourts' sayings was: "Japonaiserie for ever." Well, those docks are a famous Japonaiserie, fantastical, peculiar, unheard of – at least, one can take it in that way.' 'My studio is not bad,' he wrote in the same letter (437), 'especially as I have pinned a lot of little Japanese prints on the wall, which amuse me very much. You know those little women's figures in gardens, or on the beach, horsemen, flowers, knotty thorn branches.'

Vincent was not any happier in Antwerp than he had been in Drenthe or Neunen. Theo suggested that he should return to Brabant, but Vincent had decided to go to Paris. One morning in February 1886 Theo found a note in his office informing him that his brother was waiting for him in the Salon Carré of the Louvre. Theo had to give him a lodging in his own apartment, but as there was no studio there in which Vincent could work, he was eventually compelled to take a new apartment on Montmartre (54, rue Lepic), where for a time they settled down happily together.

But not for long. Vincent soon showed his intractability and made Theo's life a misery. 'My home life is almost unbearable,' Theo wrote to his sister, 'no one wants to come and see me any more, because it always ends in quarrels, and besides he is so untidy that the room looks far from attractive.' But he had not the heart to turn Vincent out; he continued to bear with him and to give him what Vincent most needed – respect, hope, love.

Among the artists in Paris with whom Vincent became acquainted at this period were two worthy of special mention – Emile Bernard and Paul Gauguin. Bernard, a younger man (he was born at Lille in 1868) became a true friend and did much to help Vincent in the few remaining years of his life, and much to preserve his work (both his letters and his paintings) after his death. Extracts from the letters to Bernard were first published in the *Mercure de France* shortly after Vincent's death, but not in a complete form until 1911. They are a precious addition to the letters to Theo because the two painters discuss in great detail the technical aspects of their work, and because, as an older to a younger man, Vincent felt that he could instruct Bernard. As for the friendship with Gauguin, who was five years older than Vincent, it can only be said to have been disastrous, as will be seen presently.

In the winter of this year in Paris (1887–8) Vincent's work grew in assurance and was at the same time influenced by the new developments that were taking place around him. Pissarro, Gauguin, Seurat, Toulouse-Lautrec, with all these painters he entered into intimate friendship and rivalry, and though he never compromised his own emotional convictions, his technique was improved and his whole tonality became lighter and gayer. To this period belong the famous self-portrait before the easel and many other self-portraits (*Plate 23*), the famous portrait of *Le Père Tanguy*, *The Woman with the Tambourines*, and *The Lady by a Cradle*, and many beautiful still-lifes and flower-pieces.

Then Vincent grew tired of Paris and in February 1888 made for the south. He settled in Arles and there followed a period of intense productivity. The best-known and best-loved paintings belong to this period – the *Sunflowers*, *The Chair and the Pipe*, the *Pont de l'Anglois*, the *Café at Night*, the *View of Saintes-Maries*, the *Orchard in Bloom*, the *Blossoming Pear-tree*, and the portraits of Roulin the Postman, Armand Roulin, Madame Roulin, Doctor Rey and l'Arlésienne (Madame Ginoux). His sensibility was overwhelmed by the light and colour of the south and he felt that he had to adapt his technique to render the new effects – to abandon the atmospheric nuances of the north and simplify, intensify, render the subject in all its vibrant actuality. (*Plate 25*) The self-portraits of this period reveal these same qualities.

Then Gauguin came on the scene. Gauguin wrote from Brittany, asking Vincent to intervene with Theo so that he could get some money from him. Vincent impulsively invited Gauguin to come to Arles and share his life and studio with him. Gauguin came about the middle of October and found Vincent in a state of nervous exhaustion due to overwork. Their temperaments soon clashed and by the middle of December Gauguin had decided to leave. Then, on the eve of 24 December, Vincent, in 'un accès de fièvre chaude', cut off a small piece of his ear and brought it as a gift to a woman in a brothel. The gesture was symbolic, inspired perhaps by the similar gesture of the bullfighter who cuts off a piece of the ear of the dead bull and presents it to his mistress. But the self-inflicted wound was serious. Gauguin telegraphed to Theo, who immediately came to Arles and found Vincent in hospital in a dangerous condition, and despaired of his life. But Vincent recovered and though he was in and out of hospital during the months of January and February, by 19 March 1889 he was able to resume his correspondence with Theo. Vincent's own comment on his experience was – 'to suffer without complaint is the only lesson we have to learn from life'. (*Plate 22*)

The incident had caused a great scandal in the small city of Arles, and to avoid the unwelcome attention of the curious public rather than for medical reasons, it was decided that Vincent should become an inmate of the asylum of St-Rémy, near Arles. He spent a year in this retreat, continuing to paint, but haunted by the fear of a recurrence of his mental illness. The letter to Theo in which he describes the first conception of the *Bedroom* reveals in moving detail his pathetic attempt to integrate his inner and outer worlds:

'My eyes are still tired, but then I had a new idea in my head and here is a sketch of it. . . . (*Plate 24*) This time it's just simply my bedroom, only here the colour is to do everything, and giving by its simplification a grander style to things, is to be suggestive here of *rest* or of sleep in general. In a word, looking at the picture ought to rest the brain, or rather the imagination.

The walls are pale violet, The floor is of red tiles.

The wood of the bed and chairs is the yellow of fresh butter, the sheets and pillows very light greenish-citron.

The coverlet scarlet. The window green.

The toilet table orange, the basin blue.

The doors lilac.

And that is all – there is nothing in this room with its closed shutters.

The broad lines of the furniture again must express inviolable rest. Portraits on the walls, and a mirror and a towel and some clothes.

The frame – as there is no white in the picture – will be white.

This by way of revenge for the enforced rest I was obliged to take.

I shall work on it again all day, but you see how simple the conception is. The shadows and the cast shadows are suppressed; it is painted in free flat tints like the Japanese prints. It is going to be a contrast to, for instance, the Tarascon diligence and the night café.

I am not writing you a long letter, because tomorrow very early I am going to begin in the cool morning light, so as to finish my canvas.'[4]

To the end he was to try again and again to achieve what he called 'a feeling of perfect rest', but again and again the torment and the agitation supervened – the mountains, the olive-trees, the cypresses, the sun swirling like a wheel of fire in the evening sky – all eventually conform to the same pulsating rhythm. The portraits also express his inner torment – *The Head of a Sick Man*, *The Wife of the Superintendent*, *The School-boy*, and one self-portrait. The figure of an old man seated with his clasped hands hiding his face (*On the threshold of Eternity*) is a pathetic epitome of his spiritual condition. He made many copies at this time – of Delacroix's *Pietà*, Rembrandt's *Good Samaritan* and *Resurrection of Lazarus*, and again of his favourite subjects after Millet, the *Sower* and the *Reaper*, but always giving to these subjects a peculiar intensity of his own.

In May of the next year, 1890, Theo (on the advice of Pissarro) arranged to have Vincent transferred to a hospital at Auvers-sur-Oise, an hour's journey from Paris, where he could be under the care of Dr Gachet, who had been a friend of Cézanne. Gachet was a very sympathetic physician and for a time Vincent's health was stable. Here he painted portraits of *Dr Gachet* and his daughter (*Mademoiselle Gachet at the Piano*), *A Young Peasant Girl*, *The Peasant*, *The Mairie at Auvers*, a self-portrait, and many fine landscapes and garden-scenes. For a few weeks he seemed to be happy, but his stability was very precarious. The final crisis came with tragic suddenness. On 27 July he tried to kill himself with a revolver. He lingered for two days but died on the morning of the 29th and was buried in the cemetery at Auvers.

As I have already said, there has been much discussion about the nature of Vincent's illness, and Dr Kraus's admittedly vague description – psychogenic attacks on a psychopathic basis – is as clinical as we need be. It is important to emphasize that his normal condition was perfectly sane, and that the psychogenic attacks were intermittent. In his last letter to his mother (II, 650), written from Auvers a few days before his death, he describes himself as 'quite absorbed in the immense plain with wheatfields against the hills, boundless as a sea, delicate yellow, delicate soft green, delicate violet of a dug-up and weeded piece of soil, chequered at regular intervals by the green of flowering potato plants, everything under a sky of delicate blue, white, pink, violet tones,' and adds: 'I am in a mood of nearly too much calmness, in the mood to paint this.' And in the last letter to his brother, found on him on 29 July, he wrote – 'Well, my own work, I am risking my life for it and my reason has half-foundered because of it. . . .' It had by then wholly foundered – such intensity of sensation could not be sustained by a mind so delicately balanced. But the intensity is nevertheless an index of his aesthetic sensibility, and is not itself a symptom of alienation. It is a widely accepted error that associates genius with madness. Vincent's genius was the product of two factors – a trained sensibility and a sympathetic imagination. The one factor gave him at great pains the ability to give form to the feelings aroused by the other factor. His life was one long quest for a *style*, which Goethe was the first to define correctly as the quality in art which rests on the deepest foundations of cognition, on the inner essence of things (cf. *Jubiläumsausgabe*, Cotta, 1902, vol. 33, 56–7). This inner essence of things was Vincent's life-long quest, and his final achievement.

By birth and tradition Vincent was a Northern artist. He himself was quite clear about his affinities – he was with his countrymen Hals and Rembrandt. Of Hals he said (in a letter to Bernard III, B13) – 'He painted portraits, and nothing, nothing else. Portraits of soldiers, gatherings of officers, portraits of magistrates assembled to debate the affairs of the Republic, portraits of matronly old ladies with pink or sallow skins, wearing white caps and dressed in black satin or wool, who discuss the budget of some orphanage or almshouse. He painted the portrait of many a good bourgeois surrounded by his family, husband, wife and children. He painted the drunken toper, the haggish old fish-wife in gay mood, the pretty gypsy tart, babies in their diapers, the dashing, self-indulgent nobleman with his moustache, top-boots and spurs. He painted himself, together with his wife, young, deeply in love, seated on a bench on a lawn after their wedding night. He painted vagabonds and laughing urchins, musicians too and a great fat cook.

'He did not know greater things than that, but it is certainly Dante's Paradise, or Michelangelo or Raphael, or even the Greeks. It's as beautiful as Zola, healthier as well as merrier, but as true to life, because his period was healthier and less dismal. . . .

'Hammer into your head this master Frans Hals, a painter of all kinds of portraits, the immortalizer of a whole vital and dazzling republic. Then hammer into your head the other no less great and universal master of portraiture from the Dutch Republic – Rembrandt Harmensz van Rijn, a broad-minded and very natural man, as healthy as Hals himself.'

Such was Van Gogh's own ideal – the depiction of humanity. But in a certain sense humanity failed him, for there was no unity in the civilization into which he had been born. His work therefore lacks the single-mindedness of a Hals or a Rembrandt – the limitation that is often the condition of the highest genius. He was compelled to turn from the human scene with all its injustice to contemplate 'the too great calmness' of nature. But for this too he had beloved masters from the Dutch Republic – Vermeer and Ruysdael.

'The too great calmness of nature' – that phrase indicates the alienated nature of expressionism, and in this sense Vincent was an expressionist, the greatest of all expressionists. But alienation does not conflict with but rather gives passionate force to the aim of the artist, which is to impose a unity or order on the multiplicity and confusion of his feelings. Always in Vincent's work there is this drive to order, to formal unity, but it must be understood as an order distinct from the natural order. For the order assumed by the artist's perceptions and sensations need not necessarily be the order of nature. With Wilhelm Worringer we must distinguish between Nature and the Laws of Nature. Nature is the whole realm of existence and experience, and from our observation of this realm we may derive various hypotheses

about the structure of reality. These hypotheses do not correspond to the total reality, to reality itself, which consists of spirit
as well as of matter, and, indeed, of matter still beyond the reach
of our knowledge. It is above all the spiritual aspects of reality
that seek expression in art. Vincent in his letters was always
making this same distinction: for example – '. . . *studies* done in
the open air are different from pictures which are destined to
come before the public. In my opinion, the latter result from the
studies, yet they may, in fact must, differ a great deal from them.
For in the picture the painter gives *a personal idea*; and in a study
his aim is simply to analyse a bit of nature – either to get his
idea or conception more correct, or to find a new idea . . . [my
italics].

'I consider making studies like sowing, and making pictures
like reaping.' (I, 460.)

Or from another letter of this same year 1882:

'*I do not know myself* how I paint (it). I sit down with a white
board before the spot that strikes me, I look at what is before my
eyes, I say to myself, that white board must become something;
I come back dissatisfied – I put it away, and when I have rested
a little, I go and look at it with a kind of fear. Then I am still
dissatisfied, because I still have that splendid scene too clearly in
my mind to be satisfied with what I made of it. But I find in my
work an echo of what struck me, after all. I see that nature has
told me something, has spoken to me, and that I have put it down
in shorthand. In my shorthand there may be words that cannot
be deciphered, there may be mistakes or gaps; but there is something of what wood or beach or figure has told me in it, and it is
not the tame or conventional language derived from a studied
manner or a system rather than nature itself.' (II, 448.)

Such is the aim of the alienated artist: to reveal the secret of
nature, to interpret the spirit of nature, and for this purpose to
use a language that corresponds to the experienced reality and
not to the conventions of language and scientific method. The
result is the style we call expressionism.

Expressionism is not a betrayal of nature, least of all a denial
of our human nature. Rather it is an attempt to humanize nature,
and those who accuse the modern artist of 'dehumanizing art',

or of failing to maintain a human measure or a human standard of values, are themselves denying what is most human in humanity, our capacity to transcend appearances, our ability to assert spiritual values in a world of fact. What is human in an artist is not his ability to depict humanity, nor even his ability to impose human values like restraint or dignity or nobility on the complexity of the visible universe: his duty, his simple duty, is, as Cézanne said, to be humble in the presence of nature, or, as Vincent said, to be fearful in the presence of nature. Then nature will speak through what is most natural in the artist, his sensations and feelings, his 'personal idea'.

From the point of view of an artist like Vincent, the spirit is transcendent: there exists in man a vital force, a transforming energy, that moulds every perception in the shape of a visionary or imaginative reality. Unless we concede to the imagination of the artist this 'shaping power', we can never for a moment understand the place of art in the history of mankind; we can never for a moment comprehend its variety and complexity, or its function in the evolution of human consciousness.

VIII

The Sculpture of Matisse: Balance, Purity, Serenity

Some excuse may be needed for including in this volume an essay devoted to the *sculpture* of Matisse, rather than his painting or his work as a whole. His graphic work is also significant, even from my present point of view. He told William Liebermann in 1948 that 'My drawing is the most direct and purest translation of my emotion. This is made possible by simplification of the media. I have the feeling that my emotion expresses itself through the medium of plastic writing. As soon as my line – inspired, so to speak, with a life of its own – has moulded the light of the empty sheet without destroying the tender whiteness of the paper, I stop. I can no longer add or change. The page is written, no correction is possible'.[1]

If the assumption underlying the general approach to art in this volume is accepted, then the practice of art is one of the means (in my opinion the most effective) which make it possible to redirect the aggressive instincts of man into channels of reconciliation and pacification (see pages 29 to 39). Of all the plastic arts sculpture is probably more effective than the others because it involves the artist in a direct attack on a three-dimensional solid material. Matisse's remarks on sculpture, some of which I shall quote presently, make this particular kind of emotional involvement very clear, and we shall see the same kind of involvement in the case of Henry Moore. Sculpture, properly understood and practised, is a total 'adventure', and engages the whole body, either directly or empathetically, in a muscular struggle, a co-ordination of stresses which in relation to the material, stone or clay, are aggressive, and in relation to the result aimed at, pacific and reconciliatory. A balance has been achieved between opposing forces (gravity and grace) and in the effort instinctive energies that are fundamentally aggressive become transformed. Matisse himself has said: 'There are two ways of expressing things; one is to show them crudely, the other is to evoke them artistically. In abandoning the literal representation of movement it is possible to reach toward a higher ideal of beauty. Look at an Egyptian statue: it looks rigid to us; however, we feel in it the image of a body capable of movement and which despite its stiffness is animated. The Greeks too are calm; a man hurling a discus will be shown in the moment in which he gathers his strength before the effort or else, if he is shown in the most violent and precarious position implied by his action, the sculptor will have abridged and condensed it so that balance is re-established, thereby suggesting a feeling of duration. Movement in itself is unstable and it is not suited to something durable like a statue unless the artist has realized the entire action of which it represents only a moment'.[2]

All movement, in the sense implied (the movement of throwing the discus, for example) is aggressive, and Matisse here describes exactly how sculpture functions as a diversion of the aggressive instincts.

Both painting and sculpture are 'plastic' arts, and are called such because the concern of the artist is to render the three-dimensionability of objects. This elusive quality is perhaps more easily obtained in works of sculpture which inevitably occupy space, but even sculpture can be flat and inert. The painter achieves an effect of plasticity by tonal contrasts, especially those created by the representation of light and shade. With the advent of impressionism the painter renounced chiaroscuro, an easy but obvious and essentially unrealistic method of producing a three-dimensional effect: he had then to rely on tonal contrasts alone. Although the Impressionists were prestidigitorial in their solution of the problem, a feeling of dissatisfaction remained, and was only finally resolved by Cézanne after a lifetime of struggle. Cézanne's

mature method was to 'model' the actual pigment by brush-
strokes which take the form of planes so organized in block-like
shapes that the pattern they make 'seems' solid. These shapes are
often reinforced by lines or hard edges, until the composition has
the appearance of a hewn-out quarry, or, more positively, one of
those Egyptian or Indian temples hewn out of a rocky mountain.
Hence the familiar description of Cézanne's style as 'sculptural'.

Matisse's debt to Cézanne has never been in question: 'Cézanne
was the master of us all,' he used to say. In 1899, perhaps incited
by Pissarro, he had bought the *Three Bathers* from Vollard, and
this painting hung in his studio until he gave it to the Musée de la
Ville de Paris in 1936. In a letter to Raymond Escholier, director
of the museum (and author of an intimate account of Matisse's
development as an artist), Matisse wrote:[3]

'Allow me to tell you that this picture is of the first importance
in the work of Cézanne *because it is a very solid, very complete
realization* of a composition that he carefully studied in various
canvases, which, though now in important collections, are not
the studies that culminated in the present work.

'I have owned this canvas for thirty-seven years and I know it
fairly well, I hope, though not entirely; it has sustained me
spiritually in the critical moments of my career as an artist; I
have drawn from it my faith and my perseverance: for this
reason allow me to request that it be placed so that it may be
seen to the best advantage. For this it needs both light and perspective. It is rich in colour and surface and only when it is seen at a
distance is it possible to appreciate the sweep of its lines and the
exceptional sobriety of its relationships.'

At the same time, and as part of the same deal with Vollard,
Matisse acquired a plaster bust of Henri Rochefort by Rodin
which he had seen at Vollard's. This work may not be very
significant in relation to Matisse's own sculpture, but what is
significant is that it was in this same year, 1899, that Matisse made
his first experiment in sculpture. This was a 'free copy of a piece
by A. L. Barye, a bronze representing a *Jaguar Devouring a Hare*'.
Barr describes the extraordinary persistency with which Matisse
worked on this piece: 'For many months during 1900 he worked

30   *Matisse.   Reclining Nude I.   1907*

31   *Matisse.   Reclining Nude II.   1927-9*

32 *Matisse. Head of Jeanette I.* 1927-9

33 *Matisse. Head of Jeanette III.* 1927-9

36 *Matisse. Back I.* 1909

37 *Matisse. Back II.* 1913

34 Matisse. Head of Jeanette IV. 1927-9

35 Matisse. Head of Jeanette V. 1927-9

38 Matisse. Back III. 1914-17

39 Matisse. Back IV. 1930

40   *Matisse. Tiari with Necklace.* 1930

41   *Michelangelo.*
Rondanini Pietà.
Until 1564

42   *Moore. Mother and Child.* 1931

43   *Moore. Mother and Child.* 1938

44 *Moore. Two Women with Children in a Shelter.* 1941

45 *Moore. Relief No. 1.* 1959

46 *Moore. Helmet Head. No. 2. 1950*

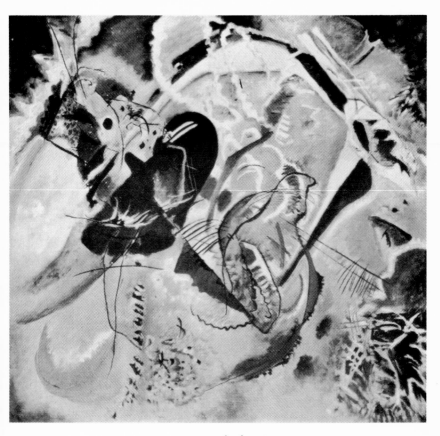

47   *Kandinsky. Improvisation 35. 1914*

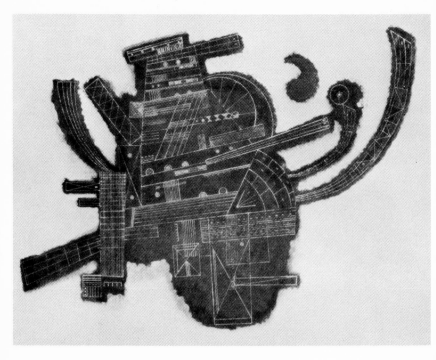

48　*Kandinsky. Green Accent. No. 623. 1935*

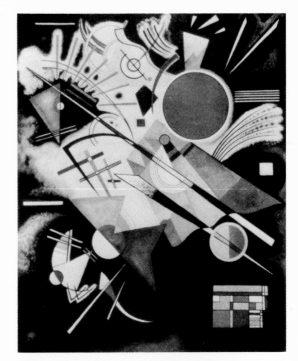

49 *Kandinsky.*
Black Accompaniment.
1924

50 *Kandinsky.*
Each for Itself.
1934

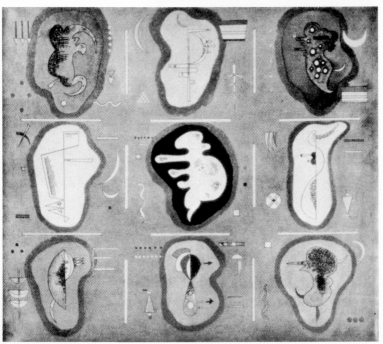

51 *Nicholson. Torre del Grillo, Rome.* 1955

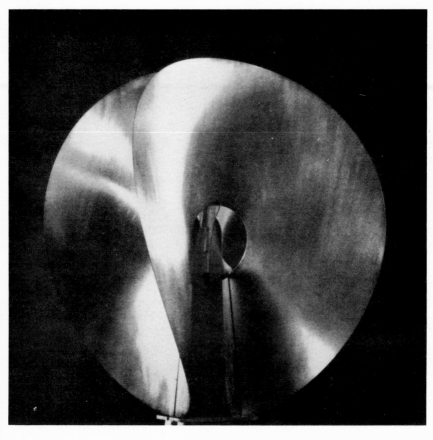

52   *Gabo. Bronze Spheric Theme. c.*1960

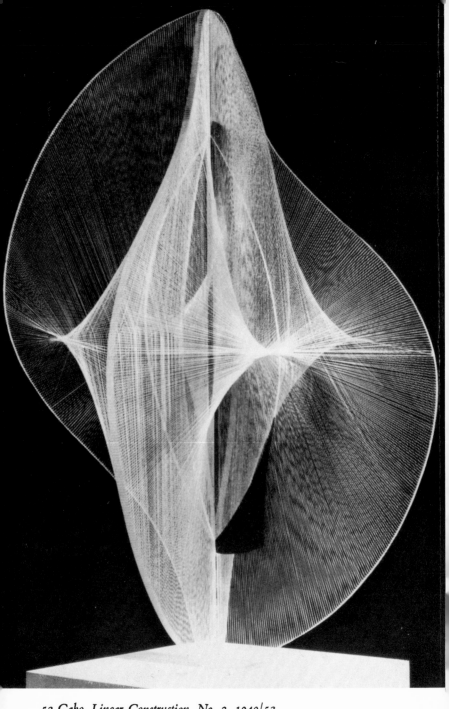

53 Gabo. Linear Construction. No. 2. 1949/53

at night at the Ecole de la Ville de Paris on the rue Etienne Marcel, a free municipal school with a studio for sculpture. Even during the period of his exhausting labour on decorations for the Grand Palais he would work from eight to ten in the evening on his Barye copy. With characteristic thoroughness he even got the body of a cat from a medical school and dissected it to study the muscles of the back and claws. The planes of muscular structure he simplified somewhat but without loss of power and tension. The *Jaguar* in its final state is a powerful interpretation of, and a magnificent homage to, Barye's masterpiece.'[4]

We should perhaps now ask why a painter like Matisse, like Degas before him and Picasso after him, should turn with such absorption to the art of sculpture. Granted, as I have already said, that both arts are concerned with plasticity as a quality to be rendered, is it likely that an attack on the problem in a medium such as bronze could help an artist whose chosen medium is paint? This is perhaps a rhetorical question which can be answered only by the artist concerned. But we may suppose that Matisse, in the spirit of Cézanne, determined to preserve the physical solidity of volumes which had been sacrificed by the Impressionists. To this end, any research that led to an understanding of volume in relation to space was essential. In this connection the story of Matisse's only direct contact with Rodin is illuminating. It was first related by André Gide in his *Journal*, but Escholier gives Matisse's own version of the story:[5]

'I was taken to Rodin's studio in the rue de l'Université, by one of his pupils who wanted to show my drawings to his master. Rodin, who received me kindly, was only moderately interested. He told me I had "facility of hand", which wasn't true. He advised me to do detailed drawings and show them to him. I never went back. Understanding my direction, I thought I had need of someone's help to arrive at the right kind of detailed drawings. Because, if I could get the simple things (which are so difficult) right, first, then I could go on to the complex details; I should have achieved what I was after: the realization of my own reactions.

'My work-discipline was already the reverse of Rodin's. But

I did not realize it then, for I was quite modest, and each day brought its revelation.

'I could not understand how Rodin could work on his St John by cutting off the hand and holding it on a peg; he worked on details holding it in his left hand, . . . anyhow keeping it detached from the whole, then replacing it on the end of the arm; then he tried to find its direction in accord with his general movement.

'Already I could only envisage the general architecture of a work of mine, replacing explanatory details by a living and suggestive synthesis.'

This last sentence gives the clue to Matisse's approach to sculpture, and, by implication, to his whole artistic method. Matisse's second piece of sculpture, *The Slave*, was a direct challenge to Rodin. It was begun in 1900 but was not finished until 1903. Its stance is exactly the same as Rodin's *St John the Baptist* (1879), though it is less than half the size and avoids the problem of accommodating the arms. The contemporary oil sketches Matisse made of the same model, one a painting in which the figure is of approximately the same height as the bronze, show the arms hanging limply down the side of the trunk. The difference between the Rodin and the Matisse is almost entirely a difference of surface treatment, but of surface reflecting not merely the local muscular tensions, but the linked succession of light and shade over the whole area of the body – a total 'adventure'. Although, as I have said, plastic volume, together with the tension between such volume or mass and the surrounding space, is the distinctive aim of the art of sculpture, Matisse believed that it could best be indicated by a 'sweep of lines' or, rather, since this phrase as applied to Cézanne's painting is hardly applicable to a piece of sculpture, by a glittering succession of integrated planes. Speaking of Maillol, whose work is the perfection of realized volume, Matisse once said that '. . . Maillol's sculpture and my work in that line have nothing in common. We never speak on the subject. For we couldn't understand one another. Maillol, like the Antique masters, proceeds by volume; *I am concerned with arabesque* like the Renaissance artists; Maillol did not like risks and I was drawn to them. He did not like adventure.'[6] (*Plate 28*)

We do not know which Renaissance artists Matisse had in mind, but probably Michelangelo for one (*Plate 27*); a plaster cast of what appears to be one of his *Slaves* appears in *Checker Game and Piano Music*, 1923; perhaps Donatello too, though I know of no mention of his *arabesque* sculpture by Matisse. What Matisse meant by *arabesque* is not in question: it is the one word that might be used, if one only were permitted, to describe his style. It implies, of course, a linear style related to Arabic or Islamic carving and calligraphy, which is essentially intricate, but the word has been used to describe the same features in art generally; for example, the *Shorter Oxford English Dictionary* refers to 'the arabesques of Raphael and the Renascence, founded on Graeco–Roman work, including representations of living creatures', and even declares that 'to this variety the term is now usually applied'. We must in any event distinguish between the stylistic and the decorative use of the term. In a superficial sense Matisse was influenced by the decorative art that he saw and admired during his visits to Algeria in 1906 and to Morocco in the winters of 1911–12 and 1912–13. On all these occasions he acquired pottery and textiles decorated with *arabesques*, and often used them in his still-lifes. But when we apply the word *arabesque* to his sculpture, we mean a formal quality independent of colour, more related to the exquisite plasterwork of the synagogues in Toledo and other cities. Matisse may have seen similar plasterwork in the mosques at Biskra or Tangier. The comparison is valid, however, only to the extent that Matisse, in his bronzes, seeks always to preserve an animated surface, a surface that reflects but subdues the play of the muscular stresses underneath. This is part of the 'living and suggestive synthesis', reinforcing 'the general architecture' of the work, the eternal stillness of its monumentality.

Nevertheless, Matisse's next piece of sculpture, the *Madeleine*, which exists in two versions (the first completed before *The Slave* in 1901, and the second, two years later), does again evoke, in its sinuosity and interflowing rhythm, the word *arabesque*, and so does the next group of bronzes, made by Matisse between 1905 and 1908. These include a *Thorn-Extractor* and a *Woman Leaning on Her Hands* (both small pieces), and a *Standing Nude*, a *Torso*

with a Head, and a *Decorative Figure* which are comparable in
scale to the *Madeleine* and *The Slave*.

It was shortly after completing this group of bronzes that Mrs
Michael Stein made notes of the instructions Matisse gave his
pupils in the *académie* that he had been persuaded to open early
in 1908. These notes, which Alfred Barr published for the first
time in his great work on Matisse, are of supreme importance for
the understanding of the principles and the methods the artist
had established for his own practice by the age of thirty-eight.
Some of his remarks on the 'study of the model' are applicable
to sculpture no less than to painting, such as 'Arms are like rolls
of clay, but the forearms are also like cords, for they can be
twisted'; or 'This pelvis fits into the thighs and suggests an
amphora. Fit your parts into one another and build up your
figure as a carpenter does a house'; or, again, 'You may consider
this Negro model a cathedral, built up of parts which form a
solid, noble, towering construction – and as a lobster, because of
the shell-like, tense muscular parts which fit so accurately and
evidently into one another, with joints only large enough to
hold their bones. But from time to time it is very necessary for
you to remember that he is a Negro and not lose him and yourself
in your construction.'

When it comes to sculpture (and here it is instructive to bear
in mind an image of the pieces Matisse himself had just made),
Matisse warns his students against having a preconceived theory
or effect with which the model must be made to agree. 'It must
impress you, awaken in you an emotion, which in turn you seek
to express. You must forget all your theories, all your ideas before
the subject. What part of these is really your own will be expressed in your expression of the emotion awakened in you by
the subject.' Always there is an interaction between perception
and conception, between the form perceived and the artist's
language of form. But sculpture has its special qualities. 'In
addition to the sensations one derives from a drawing, a sculpture
must invite us to handle it as an object; just so the sculptor must
feel, in making it, the particular demands for volume and mass.
*The smaller the bit of sculpture, the more the essentials of form must
exist.*'[7]

I emphasize this last sentence because it applies with peculiar force to the three small bronzes of 1905 and 1906. The *Little Head* especially, which is only 3¾ inches high, has a quite extraordinary suggestion of vitality. The *Torso* and the *Woman Leaning on Her Hands* in their rhythmic vitality lead directly to the larger pieces. The *Standing Nude* might be profitably contrasted with one of Maillol's small bronzes, though there is no relevant piece of the same or an earlier date. Maillol once quoted Matisse's description of the *Venus de Milo* as 'a young girl who puts herself forward', and that was Maillol's idea; his figures assert a natural exuberance. But Matisse's *Standing Nude* is not exuberant in this sense; she expresses a natural lassitude, or the modesty of a young girl who exposes her body passively. There is no attempt at classical elegance: the arms hang limply against the thighs, the feet are disproportionately large. But the form is coherent, and one rhythm, from coiled hair to heavy feet, binds it in inexorable unity.

This subordination of natural elegance to expressive rhythm is still more evident in the *Decorative Figure*. (*Plate 26*) It is not obvious why Matisse should use the word 'decorative' to describe this piece, unless he implied that rhythm is itself a decorative element. It is certainly, in this example, *arabesque*: the body itself is serpentine, the arms and the crossed legs interweave like plaited coils. The oversize head, the disproportionate hands and feet, seem to be more 'expressionistic' than any of the paintings of this same year (which incidentally include a *Still-Life* in the Yale University Art Gallery in which can be seen a plaster maquette for the *Standing Nude*), though the piece may be compared with the famous *Self-Portrait* now in the Copenhagen Art Museum, originally acquired by Michael and Sarah Stein late in 1906. But by 1907 the expressionism of sculpture and painting begin to coincide: the *Blue Nude* (souvenir of Biskra) and the *Reclining Nude I*, which were both executed at Collioure in the early months of 1907, are versions in the two media of an identical theme. Here, better than anywhere, we discern the intimate relationship between the two approaches to the problems of form. It is significant that the sculpture preceded the painting. According to Barr,[8] 'while modelling, he wet the clay too freely so that when he turned the stand the figure fell off on its head and was ruined. Exasperated, he began to paint the figure instead.' The painting then became a study for the sculpture and the result was the bronze we know, one of Matisse's masterpieces. As Alfred Barr says: 'That Matisse himself found the *Reclining Nude* exceptionally interesting is proved by the fact that for years after it was done, and far more often than any other piece of sculpture, he incorporated it as an important compositional element in his paintings.'⁹ (*Plate 30*)

It should perhaps be noted that this was the year in which, according to Gertrude Stein,¹⁰ Matisse introduced Picasso to African sculpture – an event with immediate and far-reaching effect on the future development of European art.

Matisse was now fully committed to an expressionist style in sculpture, and I would emphasize once again that it is in his modelled bronzes that he gives much the freest rein to this extreme in his style. Whether 'expressionist' is the correct word to use to describe Matisse's style is perhaps an open question. 'To dream, that is the whole thing, and to act with precision while dreaming,' is Georges Duthuit's admirable definition of the style of Matisse, and in all this, he adds, 'there is not a trace of expressionism. . . . The spectacle is neither beautiful nor ugly; there is no spectacle, only a movement, an obstacle race whose goal is, in itself and projected outside itself, motion in liberty.'¹¹ Nevertheless, there is in Matisse's work an element for which a psychological explanation is available, and it is the explanation that has been offered for expressionism in art. Alfred Barr, in one of his notes, mentions the researches of Ludwig Münz and Viktor Löwenfeld.¹² These researches show that in modelling clay the artist's hands unconsciously respond to 'inner', somatic sensations; in the process of modelling the artist gives prominence to those details in his composition which correspond to 'haptic' sensations. Such expressive emphasis is most evident in the modelling done by blind children, but it is not necessary to be blind to allow this emphasis to appear when the aim of the artist is 'motion in liberty'. This very freedom in the hand will be 'expressive'. Or, as Duthuit himself writes, 'Painting will no longer be a *means of expression*, it will be *expression*, or rather, expression and means will be one and the same thing.'¹³ This is equally true of sculpture. But expression that suggests 'a feeling of duration', a moment of rest.

Matisse now approached his most monumental task in sculpture. There was some early confusion in the dating of the four large *Bas Reliefs*, commonly known as *The Backs*. (*Plates 36–9*) The Matisse family now dates the first version 1909, which places it in the midst of the remarkable outburst of sculptural activity of the years 1908–11. It began quietly enough with the *Two Negresses* and *Seated Figure, Right Hand on Ground*, which were notable for their uncompromising plasticity; no concession is made to the inherent qualities of the metal: they are direct reproductions of figured clay. Then comes *La Serpentine*, so radical a departure from the classical tradition to which the subject and pose relate it that it was at first regarded as a caricature, but is now seen as a decisive 'happening' in the history of modern sculpture. But it merely transposes into sculpture the rhythmic inventions that Matisse had made in the same year in his famous paintings of the *Dance*. It is true that the *Dance* represents, more than any other work of Matisse's, 'motion in liberty', and that *La Serpentine* represents on the contrary a figure in languid repose; it is also true that the bodies of dancers in the painting are of natural proportions whereas the body of *La Serpentine* has calves thicker than thighs and thighs thicker than the trunk. Nevertheless, the rhythmical intention is the same: to 'thin' and compose the forms 'so that the movement would be completely comprehensible from all points of view'. I believe that the distortions can be explained by the haptic theory already mentioned; all violence is subordinated to the dominant rhythm. (*Plate 29*)

The *Five Heads of Jeanette* represent progressive stages in significant deformation. *Jeanettes I* and *II* are 'realistic', though *II* shows a general softening of the features (eyebrows, eyelids, and hair). *Jeanette III* is already decisively stylized: the hair broken into 'knobs', the eyes enlarged and protruded, the cheekbones heightened, the nose made prominent; it is also twice the size of the preceding busts. In *IV* and *V* all these tendencies are progressively enhanced: the hair gradually reduced to one 'hank', the eyes in their bony sockets greatly enlarged, all the planes simplified and given the power of a mechanical thrust. (*Plates 32–5*)

Before discussing the significance of this 'progressive deformation', we should look at the comparable evolution of the *Bas Reliefs* (*The Backs*). These reliefs, each approximately 74 inches high, represent four progressive simplifications of the same theme – the back of a nude woman seen against a wall. There is an interval of more than twenty years between the first treatment and the final one (1930). *II* is now definitely dated 1913, and was not cast until 1956. *III* is dated 1916–17, and *IV* remained unexhibited until after the death of Matisse. The series of four *Bas Reliefs* was first shown together at the Henri Matisse Retrospective Exhibition in Paris in 1956.[14]

'Deformation' is perhaps not the right word to use in describing the progressive stages of Matisse's treatment of this motive. What is involved is again a process of simplification and concentration, each version becoming more powerful in its impact. Significant is the introduction in *Bas Relief III* of long, falling hair which merges with the head. In the final version it is seen to be an essential counterthrust to the upraised shoulders and arm. The combined effect of the four *Bas Reliefs* when exhibited side by side is as powerful as anything in the whole range of modern sculpture.

The last considerable group of sculpture (apart from a bronze *Head of Marguerite*, 1915–16, and three minor bronzes of 1918) was produced in the years 1925–30. It begins with the *Large Seated Nude* of 1925, one of Matisse's finest bronzes. It is closely related to the oil painting of the *Odalisque with Raised Arms* of 1923 (Chester Dale Collection) and two lithographs, *Seated Nude with Arms Raised*, of 1924 and 1925. (Two charcoal drawings of the same subject also exist.) Once again we see how the technique of modelling imposes a certain simplification and even geometricization on the artist; it looks as though the final planes had been shaved off by a knife. The painted nude leans against an armchair; the bronze nude leans against nothing and seems to be precariously balanced on a round tuffet. As Alfred Barr remarks, it would have been easy for the sculptor to have corrected this lack of balance; but it seems to me that his intention was to isolate the body so that the spectator can better appreciate the formal *arabesque* of the 'pose'. This *arabesque* is further developed in *Reclining Nude II* of 1927–29 (*Plate 31*) and *III* of 1929, which are sequential to the *Reclining Nude I* of 1907 already discussed. That Matisse should have taken up this same theme after twenty years shows that it held some special fascination for him, and again one resorts to the ambiguous word *arabesque*. It is an *arabesque* movement of interflowing limbs and torso, an anticipation of Henry Moore's extensive development of the same motif. There is also an emanation from these figures of that feeling of languor and bodily ease which, as we know from various statements he made, was one of Matisse's ideals in art.

The *Venus in a Shell*, of which two versions exist (1930 and 1932), belongs essentially to the same group; it is a vertical exploitation of the same *arabesque*. Very different is the *Henriette, Second State* of 1927, which has the compactness and dignity of a Roman sculptural portrait; it is a powerful work that does not seem to have much relation to the rest of Matisse's sculpture. Nor, for very different reasons, does the *Tiari* of 1930 (done on his return from a voyage to Tahiti). The 'tiari' from which the piece takes its title is a large tropical flower Matisse had seen on his travels, but it is transformed into a female head, not so very different from *Jeanette IV* in its general configuration, yet carried to a degree of fantasy very rare in Matisse's work. (There are three versions of the *Tiari*, one with a necklace.) (*Plate 40*)

The only remaining piece of sculpture made by Matisse in his lifetime is the Christ for the altar of the Chapel at Vence as part of a complete décor (his designs were finished early in 1950). He is said to have studied the Christian iconography of the subject before attempting this particular task, but in the end the design was original enough, though not unlike the attenuated bronze figures of Christ found in West German bronze sculpture and enamels of the eleventh and twelfth centuries. It takes an appropriate place in the general decoration of the Chapel, but is not in itself a characteristic example of Matisse's sculpture.

An important part was played by Matisse's sculpture in his total *œuvre*. It has been asked whether Matisse made a very significant contribution to the development of modern sculpture as a whole. It is difficult to detect any influence of his work on his contemporaries or followers which could not as reasonably

be attributed to Degas, Rodin, or Maillol, yet Matisse was perhaps the first sculptor to use the expressive deformations that
have become so characteristic of sculpture in the past fifty years.
But this aspect of his work has found its detractors. For example,
Jean Selz accuses Matisse of not being quite certain of his intentions: 'He seems to waver between an impressionistic modelling,
resembling that of Bonnard's few little sculptures, and a style of
distortion rather like that of Picasso.' What I have described as
'progressive stages in significant deformation' in the five *Heads
of Jeanette*, Selz sees as signs of uncertainty or hesitation. Many
of Matisse's smaller figures, and especially his nudes, Selz writes,
'are marred by an uncouth flabbiness which is not counter-
balanced by the charm of a deliberately rudimentary modelling
technique. The play of volumes and planes lacks that balance, or
calculated imbalance, which is the mark of a really great sculptor.'
He even accuses Matisse of an 'obvious lack of sensuality'.[15]

It will be seen from what I have written above that I cannot
agree with these opinions. The 'distortion' criticized by Selz is
an intentional device, as I have explained, and the imbalance is
certainly calculated. What Selz calls 'uncouth flabbiness' is presumably the quality of 'relaxation' which again was a deliberate
aim of Matisse's – 'an art of balance, of purity and serenity devoid
of troubling or depressing subject-matter'. It is true that Matisse's
sculpture does not have the same 'grace' or 'lucidity' as his
paintings, but this again was deliberate. 'Charm, lightness, crisp-
ness,' he wrote, 'all these are passing sensations. I have a canvas
on which the colours are still fresh and I begin work on it again.
The colours will probably grow heavier – the freshness of the
original tones *will give way to greater solidity, an improvement to my
mind, but less seductive to the eye.*'[16] To carry that 'improvement'
still further Matisse resorted to the art of sculpture, the art of
greater solidity. 'The result is unity, and repose of the spirit.'

IX

Henry Moore: The Reconciling Archetype

There are two distinct approaches to the work of an artist. One might be called historical, or at the personal level, biographical: it places the artist in his time and circumstances, and attempts to explain his achievement in terms of his social origins, his up-bringing, and his relations with the artistic movements of his time. The other method concentrates on the art itself, as a series of formal inventions, and discusses the significance of that art from a wider point of view, a universal point of view. I have adopted the former method in relation to Henry Moore on a previous occasion;[1] on the present occasion I propose to attempt the second and more difficult method.

The justification for this second method has been well expressed by C. G. Jung. In an essay first published in Berlin in 1930 and now included in Volume 15 of the English edition of his *Collected Works*, Dr Jung warns us against the common practice of reducing the work of art to personal factors, a practice which tends to deflect our attention from the work of art and focus it on the psychology of the artist. The work of art, he insists, exists in its own right and cannot be explained in terms of a personal complex. If it has any general significance, it meets the psychic needs of the society in which the artist lives and is therefore concerned with more than the artist's own destiny. 'Being essentially the instrument of his work, he is subordinate to it, and we have no right to expect him to interpret it for us. He has done his utmost

by giving it form, and must leave the interpretation to others
and to the future.'

This statement of Jung's clearly justifies the approach I am
now going to make to Henry Moore's work, but the reader need
not fear that I shall inflict on him one more essay on the psycho-
analytical interpretation of art. In respect of Moore's work that
has already been done, and done excellently, by the late Erich
Neumann, a psychologist of genius.[2] My aim is more modest.
Accepting Jung's distinction between works of art that are based
on materials drawn from the artist's conscious life – 'his crucial
experiences, powerful emotions, suffering, passion, the stuff of
human fate in general', and works of art that come from the
hinterland of his mind, 'as if it had emerged from the abyss of
pre-human ages, or from a super-human world of contrasting
light and darkness', I shall assume that Moore's work is of this
second, visionary kind and I shall try to give a reasonable explanation of its universal significance.

Jung's distinction between two types of artist is based on a
wider theory of a collective psyche to which the visionary type,
in moments of inspiration, has privileged access. All people have
access to such a realm in their dreams, and a work of art is like a
dream in that it presents an image from the artist's unconscious
mind and allows us to draw our own conclusions as to its meaning. An artist is a man who can represent his subjective visions in
tangible and perceptible form. 'He has plunged into the healing
and redeeming depths of the collective psyche where man is not
lost in the isolation of consciousness and its errors and sufferings,
but where all men are caught in a common rhythm which allows
the individual to communicate his feelings and strivings to mankind as a whole.'[3]

One general feature of Henry Moore's work is immediately
obvious on the most cursory survey – its confinement to relatively
few themes. Indeed, if we give a very superficial characterization
to these themes, it may well be that we shall conclude that the
greater part of his work, perhaps more than three-quarters of it,
is accounted for by no more than two themes – the reclining figure
and the mother and child. From the moment that he was sure of
himself and of his aims, Moore has concentrated on these two

themes with an almost obsessional intensity. It is true that great artists in the past have often had the same obsessional limitations. Michelangelo's obsessions were of the same restricted kind, and there are artists of our own time who are even more obsessively restricted to one or two themes – Alberto Giacometti is an example who will immediately occur to the reader. But this is precisely the phenomenon to be explained, and explained in terms which do not obscure the problem.

I will first describe in more detail the nature of these obsessions in Henry Moore's case. I will then present any statements of his own which might throw light upon their significance, and finally I will attempt to give my own explanation.

Henry Moore was born in 1898, but owing to the interruption of the First World War his professional education was delayed for a few years, so that he did not complete its final stages at the Royal College of Art in London until 1924. He spent most of the year 1925 on a travelling scholarship which took him to Rome, Florence, Pisa, Siena, Assisi, Padua, Ravenna and Venice. He held his first exhibition in London in 1926, aged twenty-eight.

This first exhibition already included a figure of *Maternity* and a *Mother and Child* as well as two *Reclining Figures*, one of painted plaster which was subsequently destroyed, the other a bronze. Most of the other themes were masks, heads, busts or standing figures – that is to say, all subjects directly associated with the human figure. Moore's work has remained predominantly humanistic in this sense, and we might say that whenever he has departed from the human figure, as in a few animal motives, it has been to explore affinities or analogies with the human figure.

The human figure is, of course, the traditional motive of the art of sculpture, and only for short periods near the beginning of the history of sculpture and now in our own time has there been a variety of other motives. In the Neolithic Age the sculptor concentrated on ritual objects, axe-heads, maces, and other stylized weapons or tools used in religious ceremonies. In our own time a kind of sculpture we call 'constructivist' has been evolved which equally owes its inspiration to tools (machines and architectural structures) and which is deliberately 'non-figurative', that is to say, non-humanistic.

The Greeks were the first sculptors to concentrate almost exclusively on the human figure. The reason for this is to be found in the whole Greek 'ethos' or way of life, in which civic virtue is directly related to physical fitness, and beauty itself is identified with the ideal proportions of the human body (as the 'ideal' itself is further identified with the harmony of the universe). The wise man, according to Plato, will always be found attuning the harmonies of his body for the sake of the concord of his soul (*Republic*, X, 591). The body in Greek sculpture becomes a symbol, not only of physical perfection, but also of moral beauty – the fairest spectacle, as Plato puts it, being 'a coincidence of a beautiful disposition in the soul and corresponding and harmonious beauties of the same type in bodily form' (III, 402).

Throughout history man's ideals of beauty and of virtue have changed, but always a 'coincidence' of these two ideals has been found in the human body. In Egyptian or Gothic or Baroque sculpture the human figure is modified to accommodate different dispositions in the soul: the form given to the body in sculpture becomes a mirror of the ideals of that particular civilization or religion. Instead of an ideal of 'the beauty of reason' such as the Greeks held, other ages substitute the fear of the unknown, or a yearning for an absolute or transcendental existence, for some vital principle remote from human concerns. Our own age is anti-classical in this sense. We may appreciate the Greek ideals of harmony and serenity, but they do not 'coincide' with our conception of reality. We therefore seek in art forms that have a convincing correspondence, and such forms are not likely to bear much resemblance to the forms of Greek sculpture. Yet still the human body remains the best 'mirror' of the reality we wish to represent.

From the beginning Henry Moore was aware of this necessary correspondence between art and present reality (if the word 'reality' seems to beg metaphysical questions, we may substitute 'circumstances') and in a well-known statement near the beginning of his career he declared: 'Beauty, in the later Greek or Renaissance sense, is not the aim of my sculpture'. He then offered his own explanation of this disavowal:

'Between beauty of expression and power of expression there is a difference of function. The first aims at pleasing the senses, the second has a spiritual vitality which for me is more moving and goes deeper than the senses.

'Because a work does not aim at reproducing natural appearances it is not, therefore, an escape from life – but may be a penetration into reality, not a sedative or drug, not just the exercise of good taste, the provision of pleasant shapes and colours in a pleasing combination, not a decoration of life, but an expression of the significance of life, a stimulation to greater effort of living.'

In this highly concentrated philosophy of art we have the justification for the whole of Moore's subsequent stylistic development, based on what he had already established in the first decade of his work. Though as a statement it is clear and adequate enough, there are one or two phrases that may be more significant than the simple words would suggest, so I shall offer a brief commentary on them.

The whole philosophy of art implicit in the statement depends on a fundamental distinction between *beauty* and *vitality* as the 'function' of art. This distinction, as formulated by Moore, no doubt derives from the ideas, if not the actual writings, of Wilhelm Worringer, which I, a friend of Moore, had been instrumental in propagating in England at this time (in 1924 I had edited the posthumous papers of a young English philosopher killed in the First World War, T. E. Hulme, in which Worringer's ideas were first introduced to the English-speaking public,[4] and in 1927 I had succeeded in finding a publisher for a translation of Worringer's *Form in Gothic*).[5] I am not suggesting that Moore was directly inspired by Worringer: Worringer in 1908 had intuitively discerned the nature of the revolution in art that was about to break out in Europe. He gave a theoretical formulation to ideas that were already 'in the air'. I do not think Moore would have contrasted these particular words, beauty and vitality, if he had not previously been made familiar, however indirectly, with Worringer's thesis (which is, briefly, that the history of art shows that organic harmony is not sufficiently expressive for certain societies at certain periods of history: they seek a linear, inorganic basis for an art of heightened movement, heightened expression – what Worringer calls 'the uncanny pathos which attaches to the animation of the inorganic'). But this, of course, is not an escape from 'life' – life is not necessarily serene and joyful, but in many of its aspects vigorous, urgent, restless. The Greek ideal was to impose an abstract or sensuous harmony on this blind vitality; the contrasted ideal, which we might call Gothic, accepts this vitality as a virtue in itself, as a force that stimulates man to 'greater effort', as a means of expressing 'the significance of life', of penetrating to the nature of 'reality'. No question of harmony, therefore, or of pleasure; just a question of psychological perception or penetration.

So much for the purpose of art. But sculpture is a craft and in order to fulfil the purpose of art it must conform to certain rules, or remain ineffective. What these rules are has never been stated more clearly than by Moore himself, in an article first published in 1937 and reprinted as 'Notes on Sculpture' in Volume 1 of *Sculpture and Drawings* (4th edn. 1957, pp. xxxiii–xxxv).

Though strictly technical or practical, as they must be, it will be observed that these 'Notes' begin with a clear distinction between what Moore calls the conscious and unconscious 'parts' of the mind, and that the function he ascribes to the conscious part is to 'resolve conflicts', 'organize memories' and 'prevent the sculptor from trying to walk in two directions at the same time'. The rest of the article is for the most part a concentration on the problem of form or shape. He does not begin by talking about something outside sculpture, such as physical fitness, or civic virtue, or even the beauty of reason; he talks about a perceptual problem, the problem of 'comprehending form in its full spatial existence'. The sculptor must strive continually 'to get the solid shape, as it were, inside his head'. He identifies himself with the centre of gravity of the solid shape and tries to realize, from the inside, the space that the shape is displacing. This process is sometimes called empathy, and it is the process that also takes place when a piece of sculpture is being contemplated. Shape, of course, is a very indefinite concept, and Moore next observes that some shapes are 'universal', shapes to which everybody is subconsciously conditioned 'and to which they can respond if their conscious control does not shut them off'. This is an important observation to which I shall return, but Moore admits that the forms he is most directly interested in are particular forms (such as the forms assumed by bones, shells, and pebbles, and above all the human figure). He does not give any further explanation for this preference – he assumes that it is a normal human reaction. But he does admit that the modern sculptor cannot confine himself to one form-unit, such as the human figure – he must relate and combine together into one organic whole several forms of varied sizes, sections and directions. His ideal is 'a composition which has a full form existence, with masses of varied sizes and sections working together in spatial relationship'. This somewhat Baroque conception of composition explains why, while recognizing Brancusi's historical importance in the development of contemporary sculpture, Moore finds his 'one-cylindered' forms too simple, 'almost too precious'.

Moore has some further technical observations on holes in sculpture, on the right physical size for a given idea, on the relation of drawing to sculpture, on abstraction and surrealism, but he concludes with a very significant statement which I shall not attempt to summarize:

'It might seem from what I have said of shape and form that I regard them as ends in themselves. Far from it. I am very much aware that associational, psychological factors play a large part in sculpture. The meaning and significance of form itself probably depends on the countless associations of man's history. For example, rounded forms convey an idea of fruitfulness, maturity, probably because the earth, women's breasts, and most fruits are rounded, and these shapes are important because they have this background in our habits of perception. I think the humanist organic element will always be for me of fundamental importance in sculpture, giving sculpture its vitality. Each particular carving I make takes on in my mind a human, or occasionally animal character and personality, and this personality controls its design and formal qualities, and makes me satisfied or dissatisfied with the work as it develops.'

In other words, according to Moore his sculpture is 'associational' in its purpose and content, by which he means that its form is determined by 'habits of perception' evolved throughout human history. This is the kind of human art Jung described as *visionary*, and this visionary character of the art determines with directness and intensity the formal structure given to the material. Material, so often given as a determining factor in modern sculpture ('truth to material') is thus interpreted as possessing an inherent form-potential and a particular material is selected because it has organic vitality and can express more effectively than any other material the artist's vision. The material is not exploited for its own sake, but for the sake of the 'sympathy' it displays with the visionary subject to be represented.

We are now in a position to consider why Moore selected two particular form-ideas as preferred subjects for his sculpture. It might, of course, be more exact to say that the form-ideas selected Moore; an obsession is not something we arbitrarily select – like a woman we fall in love with, there is presumably an unconscious propensity for this particular form.

The reason why, throughout the history of Western art, the human body in its natural state of nudity should have been selected as the central subject of art has often been discussed, but nowhere so perceptively as in Sir Kenneth Clark's *The Nude* (subtitled 'a Study in Ideal Form'). Sir Kenneth quotes Blake's *Descriptive Catalogue*: 'Greek statues are all of them representations of spiritual existences, of gods immortal, to the mortal, perishing organ of sight; and yet they are embodied and organized in solid marble', and this gives him the clue to the central truth, which is: 'The bodies were there, the belief in the gods was there, the love of rational proportion was there. It was the unifying grasp of the Greek imagination that brought them together. And the nude gains its enduring value from the fact that it reconciles several contrary states. It takes the most sensual and immediately interesting object, the human body, and puts it out of reach of time and desire; it takes the most purely rational concept of which mankind is capable, mathematical order, and makes it a delight to the senses; and it takes the vague fears of the unknown and sweetens them by showing that the gods are like men and may be worshipped for their life-giving beauty rather than their death-dealing powers.'[6]

Spiritual existences can, of course, be symbolized by other means – by clothed bodies, as in Gothic sculpture, by distorted bodies, as in Byzantine art or by geometricized figures as in Celtic art. But nevertheless the human body is selected because it is 'the most sensual and immediately interesting subject' and it is such a subject for reasons which surely do not need to be emphasized. Not only is it always with us, the vessel containing our life, but it is the organ of all our perceptions and feelings. But the spiritual existences of which Blake writes are not necessarily beautiful: they are 'death-dealing' as well as 'life-giving' and though most men wish to live, and even to enjoy the illusion that life is everlasting, nevertheless, if art is to penetrate to the reality of life, as Moore thinks it should, then it should fearlessly represent those 'spiritual existences' that threaten life. In a quasi-scientific language these spiritual existences would be called instincts, and if we accept Freud's hypothesis that there are two classes of instincts, we then find that he characterizes them as in effect life-giving and death-dealing. The life-instinct 'comprises not merely the uninhibited sexual instinct proper and the impulses of a sublimated or aim-inhibited nature derived from it, but also the self-preservative instinct, which must be assigned to the ego and which at the beginning of our analytical work we had good reason for setting in opposition to the sexual object-instincts. The second class of instincts was not so easy to define; in the end we came to recognize sadism as its representative. As a result of theoretical considerations, supported by biology, we assumed the existence of a death-instinct, the task of which is to lead organic matter back into the inorganic state; on the other hand, we supposed that Eros aims at complicating life by bringing about a more and more far-reaching coalescence of the particles into which living matter has been dispersed thus, of course, aiming at the maintenance of life'. Life itself is seen as 'a conflict and compromise between these two trends'.[7]

Freud's formulation of this hypothesis has been much criticized, but it seems to me that it is fully supported by the history of art, which divides itself into two such general and contrasted styles, the one endeavouring to represent life, largely through its idealization of the human body, as a spiritual existence of sensuous joy, the other endeavouring to penetrate to the reality, which is not joy but conflict, not enjoyment but tragedy. But in both styles the function of art is redemptive or reconciliatory; in the one case offering the passive delight of ideal forms, in the other case offering a tragic paradox that can be clarified and sustained but never resolved in the tension of conflicting forms.

Moore is a tragic artist in this sense. He has never sought to idealize the human body, to make it the ideal representation of beauty, a stimulus to sensuous enjoyment. It is to be 'an expression of the significance of life, a stimulation to greater effort of living'. But do such aims justify the kind and degree of distortion to which Moore subjects the human body? Are not these same aims fully expressed by a sculptor like Michelangelo with complete respect for the human body as an ideal form?

It is not quite true to say that Michelangelo did not distort the human body. Sir Kenneth Clark distinguishes even in the early works of Michelangelo a 'nervous articulation' which contrasts with 'the bland forms of antiquity'. In the *David* 'there is a ripple of ribs and muscles and, beneath it, scarcely perceptible, the ground swell of some distant storm that distinguishes the *David*'s torso from those of the most vigorous antiques'. There is the head 'on its strained, defiant neck, there are the enormous hands, and the potential movement of the pose, which force him far outside the sphere of Apollo'. As for Michelangelo's later works, so much admired by Henry Moore, in these the ideal of physical beauty is completely abandoned. 'In the *Palestrina Pietà* the distortion is so great that certain critics have doubted its authenticity. The gigantic arm and torso weigh down the body of Our Lord, so that the legs seem crushed, and almost disappear, and even the torso itself has lost its firm physical structure and becomes like some ancient rock face pitted by the weather'. This might be a description of one of Henry Moore's reclining figures! As for the *Rondanini Pietà*, 'the sacrifice of this form (the human torso), which for sixty years had been the means of his most intimate communications, gives to this shattered trunk an incomparable pathos'[8] (*Plate 41*).

It is not necessary to bring Michelangelo to the rescue of Henry Moore. I mention his work because in its later developments it foreshadows, not merely the general collapse of humanism in the later sixteenth century, but also the fact that in spite of this collapse the human body survived to become what Sir Kenneth calls 'an instrument of pathos'. Pathos is an ambiguous word, but it does imply, not only passive suffering, but, in its application to art, the direct expression of any human emotion or feeling. There is 'pathos' in the relationship between a mother and her child (*Plate 44*), and an element of pathos enters into most representations of this theme in Christian iconography. Henry Moore's representation of this theme in such early pieces as the *Mother and Child* of 1924 and several similar figures of the years 1929–30 is pathetic in this sense: the stress is on the human bond of affection between mother and child, and this is still true of the monumental group carved in 1943–4 specially for a Christian setting (the *Madonna and Child* in the church of St Matthew, Northampton). But already Moore is experiencing a conflict between the pathetic and the symbolic, between the particular and the universal. In a letter explaining his aims in this work he tells us that 'there are two particular motives or subjects which I have constantly used in my sculpture in the last twenty years; they are the "Reclining Figure" idea and the "Mother and Child" idea. (Perhaps of the two the "Mother and Child" has been the more fundamental obsession.) I began thinking of the *Madonna and Child* for St Matthew's considering in what ways a "Madonna and Child" differs from a carving of just a "Mother and Child"—that is, by considering how in my opinion religious art differs from secular art'. Moore then confesses that he does not find it easy to describe this difference 'in words'; he can only suggest that a Madonna and Child should have qualities like austerity and nobility, and some touch of grandeur ('even hieratic aloofness') that would be missing in an 'everyday' Mother and Child. In other words, pathos should be excluded. But the Northampton *Madonna and Child* is almost unique in Henry Moore's work, and though nobility and grandeur are words that can be used of most of his work, austerity and aloofness are missing from what is most characteristic.

It should perhaps be emphasized at this point that Moore himself does not belong to the introspective and self-analytical type of personality. He is not, except in a very general way, familiar with the theories and terminology of modern psychology or aesthetics. A critic is therefore justified in interpreting, or giving extension to, his rare and sometimes cryptic statements of his aims. For example, in the words just quoted he uses phrases such as 'fundamental obsession' and 'hieratic aloofness' that can be given a much wider significance while yet remaining still relevant to the work under consideration. It is at this point that we must resume contact with certain findings of depth psychology and see to what extent they illuminate Henry Moore's 'fundamental obsessions'.

Personal obsessions of a neurotic kind are usually ascribed to some mental conflict whose real nature has been suppressed or disguised. An artist's obsession with a particular motive or form is not usually of this kind, and 'obsession' may be a confusing word to use in such a connection. The motive the artist selects may have some personal significance for him, but such a motive only becomes generally significant, and on that account a work of art, if it captures what Jung called, in the passage already quoted, 'a common rhythm'. It is this common rhythm that enables the artist, through his work, 'to communicate his feelings and strivings to mankind as a whole'.

It is possible to interpret this common rhythm in purely materialistic terms – that is to say, as an aesthetic quality induced by metrical harmonies and proportions. Such works of art are necessarily of universal significance – the appeal of abstract art is of this kind, and an abstract element may be said to be present like a skeleton in every artistic 'body'. But when the body is human the rhythm awakens feelings and associations that are no longer objectively harmonic ('attuning the harmonies of the body for the sake of the concord of his soul', as Plato said); on the contrary, in visionary art they may be combined with feeling and associations that are essentially demonic. But there are good demons as well as bad demons – demons that promote life and demons that destroy life. There are demons that preside over the propagation of the species and others that ensure the fertility of animals and plants. There are demons that guarantee the immortality of the soul (guardian angels) and demons that would snatch the same soul to hell (devils). But these demonic forces are not always personified; sometimes they exist merely as *tendencies* in the mind, and as such they motivate dreams and myths. To such innate tendencies Jung gave the name *archetype*, and he defined the archetype as 'an inherited *tendency* of the human mind to form representations of mythological motifs – representations that vary a great deal without losing their basic pattern. . . . This inherited tendency is instinctive, like the specific impulse of nest-building, migration, etc., in birds. One finds these *représentations collectives* everywhere, characterized by the same or similar motifs. They cannot be assigned to any particular time or region or race. They are without known origin, and they can reproduce themselves even where transmission through migration must be ruled out.'9

The Mother and Child is one such archetype, and the Reclining Figure is another. The Mother and Child motif appears first in prehistoric times; it persists all down the ages and the more it is stylistically transformed, the more it remains the same thing – an archetype of motherhood, of fertility, of the earthly propagation of the human species. Only a motif with this fundamental significance could have persisted for so long without becoming exhausted, without dying of inanition. It is sometimes stylized to such a degree that it is difficult to recognize its significance, and it is sometimes (often in recent times) so sentimentalized that it loses all significant power. But then comes a great artist, such as Giotto, or Michelangelo, or Henry Moore and restores the motif to its primordial significance. (*Plates 42, 43, 45*)

The Reclining Figure motif is not so recognizable as an archetype, but it undoubtedly is one. Moore had discovered this motif early in his career – I have already mentioned the *Reclining Woman* of 1926. But about this time, on one of his visits to Paris, which took place almost annually from 1923 onwards, he saw a replica of the Mexican reclining figure known as Chac Mool, in Mayan religion the god of rain and organic fertility, on whose flattened torso (stomach) sacrifices were offered. Moore's great series of Reclining Figures followed from 1929 onwards to the present day, and in all its transformations the motive remains archetypal. But significantly Moore changes the sex of the figure, and introduces the suggestion of human fertility, which is then merged into an Earth symbol, the female body taking on the contours and rhythms of a mountain range. Sometimes the body is excavated and within the hollow appears an internal form, a foetus. Finally the figure is divided, first into two and then into three separate forms, cliff-like and monumental, but related essentially to vital forces and to the altar upon which they are sacrificed to propitiate an Unknown God.

All Moore's other works are related more or less nearly to these two central archetypal motifs. Some are explorations of bones or skulls (*Plate 46*); sometimes the mother figure is deprived of the child and at other times a second child is added, and even a father to form together a Family Group. Sometimes the reclining figure merges into another to form an Upright Motif, which in its turn approximates to another archetypal motif, the Cross or Crucifixion. Moore's inventive spirit is like a fountain that is never still, that is always changing its form, and yet remains the same fountain, the Fountain of Life.

The Mother and Child motif is not so much propitiatory as celebrative. It takes the miracle of creation for granted, as not requiring a sacrifice to divine powers but rather a thanksgiving. The mother is idealized, becomes the Great Mother, the goddess of human fertility or fecundity; the Child is the symbol of genetic promise and continuity, of life renewed in each generation. In Christian iconography the Great Mother is the Mother of God and the Child is God incarnate, and both are 'hieratically aloof'. But as an archetype the Mother and Child is not confined to the Christian religion: it is universal and is represented in the iconography of many religions. How universal it is may be learned from Erich Neumann's analysis of the archetype,[10] which is illustrated with reproductions from the Neolithic Age, from Ancient Egyptian, Mesopotamian, Cycladic, Minoan, Greek, Etruscan, Roman, African, Mexican, Peruvian and many other cultures.

Several aspects of the Mother and Child archetype may be distinguished: the Archetypal Feminine as deity; the Feminine force in Nature as opposed to the Masculine; the Feminine as the Great Mother indissolubly bound to the Child. Moore in his sculpture has represented all these aspects of the theme, but it is the mother–child relationship that obsesses him. It would be a mistake, however, to assume that Moore's approach to the subject is in any way systematic or ideological. Rather it is essentially human, and is not in need of an intellectual justification. It explores every direct aspect of the personal relationship – the instinctive dependence of the suckling child; the child clinging to the mother for protection; the child looking outward to assert its independence; the aggressive child, renouncing the breast that fed it; and finally the child reconciled in the unity of the family. All these are familiar attitudes, 'the stuff of human fate', and the artist's representation of them is based on observation, not on speculation. Nevertheless, and this is the measure of his stature as an artist, Moore always seeks the universal in the particular, and that, as Goethe once said, is the clue to the very nature of poetry, of all great art.

X

The Lucid Order of Wassily Kandinsky

As a painter Kandinsky's achievement was coherent in development, original in style, and accumulative in force; but the painting was the direct expression of a slowly matured philosophy of art. It is possible that this philosophy of art has as much significance for the future as the paintings that were its outcome, but in this essay I shall try to show how the philosophy and the painting evolved, step by step in dialectical correspondence.

Wassily Kandinsky was born on 4 December 1866, in the city of Moscow. His father belonged to a family that had for many years lived as exiles in East Siberia, near the Mongolian frontier. There seems to have been some mingling of blood in the family history: one of Kandinsky's great grandmothers is said to have been a Mongolian princess, and there was a distinct Mongolian cast on Kandinsky's own features. His mother, however, was a true Moscovite, and the son was always sentimentally attached to the city of his birth. His maternal grandmother was German, and German was a language he spoke in his infancy; he was fascinated by German fairy-tales. The Kandinskys seem to have been fairly well-to-do; when Wassily was only three he travelled with his parents in Italy. Then in 1871 they all moved to Odessa, where Kandinsky began to learn music and where from 1876–85 he went to school. At the end of this period it was decided that he should study law, which meant a return to Moscow. These legal studies lasted until 1892, but during this period he paid his first visit to Paris (1889), an experience he repeated as soon as he had passed his final examinations (1892). These visits to Paris seem to have been for recreation only – Kandinsky does not record any artistic experiences at this time. More significant, from this point of view, was an exhibition of the French Impressionists which he saw in Moscow in 1895. A painting by Monet was a revelation to him, and made him aware of a nascent longing to paint. In 1896 he declined an offer of a post in the University of Dorpat and went instead to Munich, determined to test his now fully awakened desire to be an artist. In 1897 he became a pupil of Anton Azbé, but did not make much progress in the academic methods of his school. There, however, he met a fellow Russian student, two years older, Alexei von Jawlensky, from whom he first heard about Van Gogh and Cézanne. In 1900 he joined the Munich Academy where Franz von Stuck had been the master of painting since 1895, and had gained considerable fame as a teacher. Von Stuck was a romantic landscape painter of the school of Böcklin, but his influence on Kandinsky was not profound. Of more significance, probably, was the movement which, originating in England, Scotland and Belgium, swept over Europe in the last decade of the nineteenth century and was variously known as the Modern Movement, Art Nouveau and Jugendstil. In Germany, Munich became the centre of this movement, and *Jugend* and *Simplicissimus*, two illustrated magazines founded in 1896, represented its spirit and style. In painting the style was represented by Munch, Hodler and Klimt, and this is the style adopted by Kandinsky in his apprentice years.

Will Grohmann, in his monograph on the artist,[1] illustrates a poster which Kandinsky designed for the first exhibition of the Phalanx, a group he himself had founded in 1901. It is in the new style, and apart from the typography typical of the movement, represents two knights with shields and lances attacking an encampment in front of a castle. The stylization is already extreme, and from this design onwards we can trace a gradual evolution of form which ends in the first completely abstract paintings of nine years later. Other influences were to be superimposed, particularly that of the French Fauves; but the argument I shall put forward in this essay is that the continuity of Kandinsky's stylistic development is unbroken from this early Jugendstil phase until the end of his life. One must therefore begin with a consideration of the formal qualities of Jugendstil or Art Nouveau.

The formal characteristics of distinct periods in the history of art have often been described, especially since Wölfflin's invention of a useful terminology; but the psychological motives that determine these morphological peculiarities are still very obscure. Following Wölfflin we can speak of linear as opposed to painterly composition, and such a linear emphasis became apparent in the last quarter of the nineteenth century. We find it manifested not only as a renewed interest in drawing as such, and in the popularity of etching and engraving among amateurs of art, but as a quality in decorative motifs of every kind – in wrought ironwork and silverware, in furniture and above all in typography. Book design, including magazines and catalogues, provides a very good index to the whole development, and in this medium one can follow the gradual transition from the naturalistic fantasies of a Beardsley or a Crane to the linear abstractions of a Van Doesburg or a Mondrian. Kandinsky's designs for catalogues and posters, for the decoration of the two books he produced at this time (*Über das Geistige in der Kunst* and *Klänge*) illustrate this same gradual transition from naturalism to linear abstraction. Nevertheless, gradual as the transition was, there came a point when abstraction *as such* was deducible from the extremes of Jugendstil, and the discovery was Kandinsky's.

It is sometimes claimed that a painter in Lithuania (Ciurlionis) or Russia (Larionov or Malevich) was the first abstract painter; in Paris they would say Picabia or Delaunay. No doubt it has many times in the past occurred to a painter that his colours might be composed like sounds in music, and many such harmonic elements exist even in classical painting. These questions of priority belong to the childish aspects of historiography; what is of serious interest is the conviction that carries a discovery through to a coherent style. Kandinsky himself was quite firm on the question of his 'priority'. In a letter to me dated 9 May 1938, describing the early days of his experiments in Munich, he wrote: 'C'était un temps vraiment héroïque! Mon Dieu, que c'était difficile et beau en même temps. On me tenait alors pour un "fou", des fois pour un "anarchiste russe qui pense que tout est permis", avec un mot pour un "cas très dangereux pour la jeunesse et pour la grande culture en général," etc., etc. J'ai pensé alors que j'étais le seul et le premier artiste qui avait le "courage" de rejeter non seulement le "sujet", mais même chaque "objet" dehors de la peinture. Et je crois vraiment que j'avais complètement raison – j'ai été le premier. Sans doute la question "qui était le premier tailleur" (comme disent les Allemands) n'est pas d'une importance extraordinaire. Mais le "fait historique" n'est pas à changer.'

One might say that once Jugendstil had reached its limit of development, the further step to abstraction was inevitable, and that no particular artist deserves the credit for a crystallization that was the impersonal outcome of the situation that existed in the first decade of the twentieth century. Kandinsky always believed that he had made an independent discovery, and he has related the circumstances. Coming home to his studio one day in 1908 he saw a painting on his easel and was thrilled by an unexpected beauty. Coming closer he saw that the painting was one he had left upside-down, and that its adventitious beauty was due to the non-representational function of the forms and colours in that position. He was already experimenting at the extreme limits of Fauvism, but he now suddenly realized that far more direct and powerful possibilities of communication were latent in form and in colour used symbolically, without any representational intention. He set about to explore these possibilities, working cautiously and testing his methods at every step. At the same time he began to elaborate a theory to justify his experiments, and this theory he set out in a thesis to which, when it was published in 1912, he gave the title *Über das Geistige in der Kunst* (Concerning the Spiritual in Art). A close study of this book is essential to any complete understanding of Kandinsky's art.

It is often objected that art needs no theoretical justification – that it is a sign of weakness in an artist to attempt any verbal exposition of his activity. If so it is a weakness many artists have felt, from Leonardo to Reynolds and Delacroix. Several modern artists, though not venturing to compose a formal treatise, have written statements or letters that give us necessary guidance as to their intentions – Van Gogh and Cézanne are examples. One of the greatest artists of our time, whom no one would accuse of intellectualism, has left us with perhaps the profoundest writings on art of all time – Paul Klee. Kandinsky did not have Klee's intensely introspective vision; nevertheless, *Concerning the Spiritual in Art* is a bold and original essay in aesthetics, written on the basis of general experience, and establishing for the first time a programme for an advance into what Kandinsky called 'an age of conscious creation'. We shall see in a moment what he meant by this phrase, but one should note that he makes very little use of the word 'abstraction', though he was familiar with Wilhelm Worringer's *Abstraction and Empathy*,[2] published by his own publisher two years before he began to write *Concerning the Spiritual in Art*. Worringer had shown that a tendency towards abstraction was one of the recurrent phenomena of the history of Northern art. Kandinsky realized that the spiritual condition of Europe was calling for another of these recurrent phases of abstraction, and more consciously, more deliberately than any other artist of the time, he decided to lead European art in this required direction.

The theory put forward by Kandinsky in his book may be summarized as follows: Art begins where nature leaves off (Oscar Wilde had said this). Art springs from an internal necessity, a need to communicate feeling in an objective form. (Nature interferes with the exactitude of such communication.) The work of art is a construction (not necessarily geometric) making use of all the potentialities of form and colour, not in an obvious way, for the most effective construction may be a hidden one, composed of seemingly fortuitous shapes – 'somehow' related forms that are actually very precisely bound together. 'The final abstract expression of every art is number', but Kandinsky recognized that the artist might be dealing with irregular rather than regular elements, and that it would therefore be difficult to translate his structure into mathematical form. The motive is always psychological – Kandinsky did not hesitate to say 'spiritual', though the German word he used, 'geistig', has not quite the same superstitious overtones as the English word. But 'the artist must have something to communicate, for mastery over form is not his goal, but rather the adapting of the form to inner significance'. The test, the standard of judgement, is always subjective – in this Kandinsky identifies himself with the expressionist theory of art. 'That is beautiful which is produced by inner need, which springs from the soul.'

There is in this theory of art an Hegelian synthesis which must be appreciated: the eternal contradiction between inner and outer, between subjective and objective, between human consciousness and an indifferent world of fact (Nature), is resolved in the unity of the work of art. Kandinsky maintained that the supreme work of art is a highly conscious construction determined by the patient elaboration of plastic forms to correspond to a slowly 'realized' inner feeling. The forms might have an arbitrary beginning – a scribble, an improvisation of line and colour; but these forms are then modified or manipulated, teased and tested, until they correspond to an even more clearly realized inner feeling – the feeling is realized as the forms achieve a correspondence – can be realized only if the artist succeeds in so disposing the forms that they express the feeling.

The 'method' that Kandinsky now adopted has been described by Grohmann and others: what at first sight seems to be the most fortuitous kind of doodling was actually a careful disposition of irregular formal elements. The first composition relying entirely on such abstract elements is a water-colour of 1910 in the possession of the artist's widow. But Kandinsky did not immediately devote all his energies to abstraction. He felt his way slowly forwards, and between 1910 and 1914 there are many compositions that clearly have a basis in naturalistic elements (*Plate 47*) (even much later, for example during the First World War when he returned to Moscow, he occasionally painted in a representational style). But there was no turning back, and after his return to Western Europe at the end of 1921 he never again returned to realism.

Kandinsky was alone at first, but he was soon to receive support from other and younger artists. During the course of 1911 he made the acquaintance of Paul Klee, Hans Arp, August Macke and Franz Marc. Of these Marc seems to have best understood Kandinsky's intentions, and together they decided to organize the group which they called 'Der Blaue Reiter' (The Blue Rider). They held their first exhibition in Munich in December of that year, and two months later, in February 1912, a second exhibition in Munich, followed later in the year by an exhibition in Berlin. This same year Klee, Marc and Macke visited Paris and made contact with Robert Delaunay, whose 'orphic' painting was also developing in the direction of abstraction. Delaunay was henceforth to keep in close touch with the Munich group, and there is no doubt that he had a considerable influence on Klee, Marc and Macke, and was perhaps in his turn influenced by the theories of Kandinsky.

The outbreak of the war brought to an end the activities of the Blaue Reiter. Kandinsky was displaced and returned to Russia via Switzerland and the Balkans. In Moscow he found two abstract movements already in existence – Suprematism under the direction of Malevich and Constructivism under the direction of Tatlin. The first two years of his residence in Moscow do not seem to have been very productive – very little work survives from this period of his life (Grohmann calls it an 'intermezzo'). In 1917 Gabo and Pevsner returned to Moscow and the next five years were devoted to politics and administration rather than to creative work. After the Revolution Kandinsky became a professor at the National Art School and in 1919 founded and directed a whole organization of central and provincial art galleries. In 1920 he was appointed Professor of Art at the University of Moscow; in 1921 he founded an Academy of Art. But the thermidorian reaction was already setting in and the official policy of 'socialist realism' was opposed to a revolutionary art. Kandinsky decided to leave Russia. By the end of the year he had reached Berlin, a city he did not find very congenial. The artistic scene was dominated by Dadaists and Expressionists, for whom Kadinsky had never much sympathy, and a spirit of desperate nihilism pervaded the intellectual life of the German capital. Luckily he received almost immediately an invitation from Walter Gropius to join the staff of the Bauhaus, the school of basic design which Gropius had directed since 1919 in Weimar. There he found Klee and Lyonel Feininger, the architect Adolf Meyer, the designer Johannes Itten, and in general an atmosphere and a policy which were completely to his liking. Kandinsky was to remain at the Bauhaus until the tragic end in 1933 – five years longer than Gropius himself, who resigned the directorship in 1928.

The Moscow 'intermezzo' and the closing of the Bauhaus by the Nazis are events that divide Kandinsky's abstract work into three distinctive periods – the Munich years (1908–14), a period of experiment and discovery; the Bauhaus years (1922–33), a period of definition and exposition; and the Paris years (1933–44), which were years of consolidation and elaboration. I have already described the formative period in Munich; I will now try to characterize the remaining periods.

Kandinsky ended his book of 1912 by announcing that 'we are fast approaching a time of reasoned and conscious composition, in which the painter will be proud to declare his work constructional', and this gives the clue to his own future development. The Constructivist movement which he encountered in Russia must have clarified his ideas and given him fresh confidence, though he seems at the time to have reacted against the severely geometrical forms of Malevich and Tatlin. The comparatively few pictures that have survived from the Moscow period, or of which photographic records exist, are continuous with the last paintings done in Europe – violently explosive forms often contained within an irregular oval outline. The shapes of the constituent elements are still vaguely suggestive of the features of a landscape, of the débris of an earthquake or a flood, but just at the end of the Moscow period a tendency towards geometric precision becomes evident – for example, the *Bunter Kreis (Varicoloured Circle)* of 1921 now in the Yale University Art Gallery. From 1921 onwards the geometricization proceeds apace, and by 1923, when Kandinsky was settled in the Bauhaus and fully productive once again, the process is complete. But if one examines a typical canvas of this period (*In the Black Square*, 1923) one can still see the skeleton of a landscape. The circles do not represent the sun, nor the triangles mountains, nor the curves clouds, but they are the archetypal elements of a landscape and suggest a deliberate refinement of such elements. 'Step by step,' Grohmann suggests, 'Kandinsky

in Moscow approached a new harder and more objective form
of composition which came as a surprise to his acquaintances
when it was first shown to them in Berlin. As in the case of
Klee, any new departure was always regarded by his friends as
a mistake.'

But Kandinsky was now sure of himself, and the Bauhaus
period is to be regarded as a period of consolidation in which a
new method and indeed a new form of art was for the first time
perfected. It was a lonely path that Kandinsky had chosen. In so
far as it was always based on fantasy – that is to say, on a free
combination of images – it had something in common with
Klee's art. But Kandinsky did not possess Klee's sense of humour,
nor Klee's essentially poetic imagination. Kandinsky's images
were always *plastic*, that is to say, elements of form and colour
that were completely divorced from sentimental associations (I
use the word 'sentimental' in its precise and not in its derogatory
meaning). This does not imply that the plastic forms have no
symbolic function; on the contrary, a line, a circle, a triangle, or
any other geometrical element, always has a reliable significance
for Kandinsky. It is true that he would sometimes give a painting
a sentimental title – *Obstinate*, for example. But this is an exception: the usual titles (*Yellow Point*, *Sharp-calm Pink*, *Quiet Harmony*,
Calm Tension, *Capricious Line*, *Contact*, *Bright Unity*, *Wavering*,
Counterweights, *Upward*, etc.) refer to physical forces or conditions. (*Plates 48, 49*) These physical elements constitute a language of forms, used to communicate a meaning, an inner
'necessity'. Kandinsky was not very precise in his definition of
this inner necessity – he seems to have regarded it as an indefinite
spiritual (or one can say psychological, or even neural) tension
which was released in the act or process of composition. There is
no doubt that he always had the analogy of musical composition
in mind, and I know no better clue to Kandinsky's method of
composition than the *Poetics of Music* by his compatriot and
fellow exile, Igor Stravinsky.[3] (There is, I believe, a close similarity between the formal evolution of these two great contemporary artists.) In the first chapter of this book Stravinsky writes:
'We cannot observe the creative phenomenon independently of
the form in which it is made manifest. Every formal process

proceeds from a principle, and the study of this principle requires precisely what we call dogma. In other words, the need that we feel to bring order out of chaos, to extricate the straight line of our operation from the tangle of possibilities and from the indecision of vague thoughts, presupposes the necessity of some sort of dogmatism.' And Stravinsky proceeds to define dogmatism as a feeling or taste for order and discipline fed and informed by positive concepts.

When he comes to deal with the composition of music, Stravinsky defines music in its pure state as free speculation. 'It is through the unhampered play of its functions that a work is revealed and justified. We are free to accept or reject this play, but no one has the right to question the fact of its existence. To judge, dispute and criticize the principle of speculative volition which is at the origin of all creation is thus manifestly useless.' Stravinsky then proceeds to maintain that 'inspiration is in no way a prescribed condition of the creative act, but rather a manifestation that is chronologically secondary.'

'*Inspiration, art, artist* – so many words, hazy at least, that keep us from seeing clearly in a field where everything is balance and calculation through which the breath of the speculative system blows. It is afterwards, and only afterwards, that the emotive disturbance which is at the root of inspiration may arise – an emotive disturbance about which people talk so indelicately by conferring upon it a meaning that is shocking to us and that compromises the term itself. Is it not clear that this emotion is merely a reaction on the part of the creator grappling with that unknown entity which is still only the object of his creating and which is to become a work of art? Step by step, link by link, it will be granted him to discover the work. It is this chain of discoveries, as well as each individual discovery, that give rise to the emotion – an almost physiological reflex, like that of the appetite causing a flow of saliva – this emotion which follows closely the phases of the creative process.'

I have quoted this passage at length because it is an exact description and explanation of Kandinsky's method of composition and indeed of his whole philosophy of art. Stravinsky once described himself (to a gendarme) as an 'inventor of music'. Kandinsky was an inventor of paintings, and both artists maintained that 'invention presupposes imagination but should not be confused with it'. Kandinsky invented his formal elements; but his creative imagination enabled him to give expressive coherence and unity to these elements.

Every apparently casual scribble or brush-stroke in a composition by Kandinsky is deliberately invented: he would spend many hours drawing and redrawing these apparently informal details, and not until they had become accurately expressive signs would he transfer them to the composition. This is what Kandinsky meant by 'conscious creation': it is identical with Stravinsky's 'principle of speculative volition', and it should not be confused with the 'informal art' that has come into existence since Kandinsky's death. This informal art (tachism, action painting, etc.) can claim some relationship to the first phase of Kandinsky's abstract development, and even to the early stage of 'improvisation' in the composition of his later compositions. What separates Kandinsky from most of the later 'informalists' is his insistence on the conscious control of the constituent elements of form and colour. Compare the difference between the disciplined structure of the atonal music of Berg and Webern and the informal expressionism of 'musique concrète'.

During his Bauhaus period, in 1926, Kandinsky set down his principles of composition in a treatise which he called *Point and Line to Plane*. This carries the theoretical exposition that forms a part of *Concerning the Spiritual in Art* to a more thorough analytical stage. The earlier book had been concerned mainly with the effect of colour in relation to form; Kandinsky now explores the dynamism of line and plane, especially in relation to the techniques of etching, wood-engraving and lithography. Horizontal and vertical are interpreted not merely as opposed directions, but also as symbolic 'temperatures': horizontal as cold, vertical as warm. In fact, a temperature or a temperament is ascribed to all linear directions and spatial areas – the bottom of a composition is an area of constraint or heaviness, the top an area of lightness and liberation. A composition thus becomes an orchestration of vital forces expressed in plastic symbols. The musical analogy is always in the background, and the concepts of time, rhythm, interval and metre hitherto reserved to music are freely introduced into the aesthetics of painting. Kandinsky's aesthetics (a total aesthetics covering all the arts) stands or falls by the justness of this analogy, and from the early days of the Blaue Reiter it was based on discussions with composers like Arnold Schönberg. (*Plate 49*)

The Paris period does not differ fundamentally from the Bauhaus period, but Kandinsky was now free to develop his art in isolation, and with a self-confidence that had been proved in ten years of pedagogic activity. There is no decisive change in the character of his painting, though new motives are frequently invented and certain 'schema', such as a division of the picture-space into self-contrasted panels or architectural 'façades', are adopted. (*Plate 50*) More remarkable, perhaps, is a certain barbaric richness of colour which seems to be a reminiscence of the indigenous art of Russia and Asia. Grohmann compares these late paintings with Mexican and Peruvian art, relying on the 'Amerasian' speculations of Strygowski for an historical link. Whether these and other similarities are due to an atavistic recollection on Kandinsky's part, or to his conscious knowledge of and sympathy for these exotic arts, is a question I would not like to decide.[4]

Since Kandinsky's death in 1944 the understanding and appreciation of his work has grown very considerably, but there is always a latent opposition to it. In so far as this opposition is part of a general failure to understand and appreciate abstract tendencies in art, it calls for no comment. But there are many sincere lovers of contemporary art, admirers say of Klee or Picasso, who are unmoved by Kandinsky's work. In the same way there are music lovers who admire Bartók or Prokofiev, but who remain unmoved by Alban Berg or Anton Webern. Perhaps the clue to this limitation lies in the word 'unmoved'.

In Kandinsky's work, as in the work of the composers I have mentioned, the emotion involved is Apollonian rather than Dionysian. 'What is important for the lucid ordering of the work – for its crystallization [I am quoting Stravinsky again] – is that all the Dionysian elements which set the imagination of the artist in motion and make the life-sap rise must be properly subjugated before they intoxicate us, and must finally be made to submit to the law: Apollo demands it.' Kandinsky's art is not for every taste; but for those who can appreciate the strength and beauty of an art that imposes the clearest intellectual unity on a chaos of Dionysian elements, his achievement will rank among the highest in the history of modern art.

XI

Ben Nicholson: The Inner Essence

There is today a tendency to abandon the idea of professionalism in art. 'Action painting' is a technique that can be practised, with distinctions only of degree, by apes as well as by men. More artists than ever before are autodidactic, and parade their amateurism as a virtue.

Spontaneity is a positive virtue, and I do not wish to decry a movement that has isolated and emphasized this virtue. I merely wish to assert that Ben Nicholson is in every sense of the word a professional artist – the son of a professional artist, familiar since his childhood with a professional environment. He was born with a paintbrush in his hand. The distinction he was to make, and no one more clearly, is that a professional artist is not necessarily an academic artist. Schools of art are institutions peculiar to the modern age: before the eighteenth century the artist learned his technique in a workshop. This is the way in which Nicholson became a painter, learning in childhood a visual mode of expression as natural as speech.

Like speech, this mode of expression is disciplined – has its syntax and grammar. It has also qualities that are more personal – tone, accent and inflexion. A successful artist (like a successful singer) is one who can give perfect pitch, volume and expressiveness to the elements of a language. In short, he achieves *style*, which is not so much the man himself as a syntax or order which the artist gives to his vision. It is a curiosity of criticism that we always tend to judge a writer by his style, but in the criticism of modern painting the concept tends to be lost. It is true that we speak endlessly about form and composition, even 'facture' and 'plasticity', but never of the fusion of all these concrete and analysable elements into an apprehension of the inner essence of things, an essence expressed in a visual language that is but a refinement of the symbolic means we all use when we wish to transfer a meaning into visible signs.

The distinctiveness of the movement in art of which Nicholson has become so exquisitely a master is indicated by the phrase I have just used – a refinement of the symbolic means that constitute a visual language. For centuries in Europe such a refinement has been subordinated to the demands of mimetic literalism, of illusionism (the parallel in literature would be an onomatopoeic use of words that subordinated meaning to the reproduction of sounds). This is not the place to make yet another excursion into the history of art for the sole purpose of justifying deviations from realism or naturalism: the autonomy of art as a formative activity is now universally recognized. What is not so easy to establish is the autonomy of the artist. We speak of the Gothic *style*, or the *style* of the Florentine School, meaning by this use of the word those elements which a number of artists have in common; but we can also mean, and more and more tend to mean, those elements which are peculiar to one artist, isolate him and make him eccentric. The desire and pursuit of the particular has been the preoccupation of the modern movement in art – against which, I believe, certain artists have consciously or unconsciously reacted. The contrary tendency, known since Plato first used the phrase to define the nature of love, as the desire and pursuit of the *whole*, might also be phrased as the desire and pursuit of the inner essence of things. Wholeness is integrity, purity, concordance; abstract qualities which are nevertheless to be expressed only in the shape and texture of visible forms. 'Expressed' – an impossible word, meaning 'squeezed out' as though the process were one of milking a cow; whereas what is involved is a harmonious construction, an object of mathematic exactitude, an inconceivably delicate instrument that corresponds to the 'deepest foundations of cognition' (Goethe's expression, 'auf den tiefsten Grundfesten der Erkenntnis'.) This correspondence is possible only to a sensibility trained to exact application and judgement.

There have not been many occasions in the history of art when such an exquisite style has been possible. It was possible in the Neolithic period, which produced ritual tools and weapons in jade and other precious stones that represent man's first intuitive recognition of formal beauty; it was possible in Greek architecture and pottery (I have always found a correspondence between Nicholson's paintings and the white-ground vases of the fifth century BC); it was possible in certain Byzantine mosaics and Gothic reliquaries and ivories; and again in the Renaissance, in the sculpture of Jacopo della Quercia and the painting of Piero della Francesca. This purity of style has been rediscovered in our time, in one or two paintings by Seurat, in the 'classical' cubism of Picasso and Braque, in Mondrian's paintings and in the sculpture of Arp, Gabo and Hepworth.

Such a 'pure' style is often called classical, but though I have been as guilty as anyone in the past of such a mistake, I believe it is an error to use historical terms like classical and romantic for the qualitative differences found in modern painting. That apprehension of the inner essence of things which I have already mentioned is possible to artists of various temperaments – perhaps it always was, and who shall say, in this respect, whether a Poussin or a Turner was nearer to success? The languages differ, but they try to express the same reality, and it is this 'desire and pursuit' which distinguishes the artist, whatever his temperament. Integrity, intensity, concentration – these are the qualities that make for success in the pursuit, and they are implements which a man can use whatever his temperament (temperament being the quality an artist surrenders to conform to a school). Nicholson, as Byron said of Shelley, is of no school, and the longer I have watched his development, the more clear it has become to me that the means he employs to reach the inner essence of things are uniquely his own. Even in the technical sense he has certain knacks (*trucs*) which are peculiar to him, such as the passionate sacrifice of innumerable razor-blades to abrade his painted surfaces to the desired degree of expressive tension. But beyond all such means (and supreme among such means is his linear grace, which again invokes Greek vase-painting) is an intuitive relationship to things-in-themselves. This, though always implicit in his non-figurative works, is made evident in his drawings from nature, an activity which has always run parallel to the process of abstraction. These drawings reveal a perfect understanding of organic form, in landscape and vegetation, as well as a sympathy for architectural form – he can seize the beauty of a temple or a tower with a single sensitive line. (*Plate 51*) They also reveal, which may not be so obvious, a sense of humour; humour also being the inner essence of certain scenes.

There are, as we know, degrees of abstraction – once the process of stylization is set going in the development of a period or of a person, the form itself begins to take command. Just as one may generalize and say that all cosmic evolution is a progress from chaos to form, so all apprehension of reality (basically chaotic when the doors of perception first open in childhood) is also a progress from chaos to form. But form, as Henri Focillon so beautifully demonstrated, once isolated and outlined, takes on a life of its own – divides, combines, extends, proliferates – and the artist has but to guide the children of his imagination towards the 'deepest foundations of cognition'. The misunderstanding of abstract art, the widespread failure to appreciate its relevance, proceeds from an inability to follow form from its origin in nature to its goal in cognition. In the stylistic progress of an artist like Ben Nicholson there is a kind of organic logic, and one could, in theory, unravel every visual syllogism. But in practice forms fuse into forms: the transitions, the melting images that we can observe in certain film techniques, have no place in the finished painting. One can trace an organic development between painting and painting, between the work of one year and the work of the next; but each single painting conceals the growth that has led to the final form.

Landscape, still-life, still-life with landscape, still-life with abstract ground, pure abstraction – all are facets of the same apprehending faculty, the same penetrating vision.

Words are clumsy instruments to describe such a vision. I have no exact terminology to define the final stage which I have called 'pure abstraction'. Forms cannot be divorced from visual experience: the circle, the rectangle, all geometric forms evolve from primary sense-data – from the habitual gestures of our arms and fingers, from the *gē* (earth) that we measure with our organs of perception. The inner essence of things is metrical, and all art is a realization and comprehension of this fact.

But we have sensibility as well as sense – feeling as well as intuition. The quality of feeling is conveyed by colour – also by form in so far as form is dynamic, that is to say, gives an illusion of movement. But above all by colour. Here, in this realm, one can only establish sympathetic relations between painter and spectator. It is true that there is a science of colour-harmonies, but a great artist can often defy it (for the sake of the discord that expresses sublime terror or awe). Nicholson is not an artist with such ambitions. Harmony and serenity are the ideals he would like to represent by his colour, and a more individual quality which I can only call coolness, which recalls the essential quality of Vermeer. When combined with pure abstraction this leads to a restraint which some people mistake for lack of passion – as though one were to say that the poetry of Mallarmé or the music of Stravinsky lacked passion. These comparisons (as *all* comparisons between the arts) are inexact – Nicholson is not so inhibited as Mallarmé nor as various as Stravinsky – but they perhaps serve to indicate the mental climate of this artist's work – its clarity, its precision, its discipline and its depth.

XII

Naum Gabo: Before the Gates of the Vacant Future

When war was declared on 1 August 1914, Naum Gabo, then a student at the University of Munich, decided to seek refuge in Scandinavia, and made his way, in the company of his brother Alexei, first to Copenhagen and then to Oslo. Gabo had left Russia in 1910 and gone to Munich to study medicine. There he had come under the influence of the great art historian Heinrich Wölfflin, and had gradually abandoned medicine for philosophy, applied science, and the fine arts. By the time he reached Norway Gabo was fully determined to become a sculptor, and there, among the Norwegian fjords, 'the real Gabo was born'. These are the words of his brother, who continues:

'During the years that we lived together in Norway, Gabo loved to think aloud, and I was his constant listener. We used to go very often for walks along the shores of the fjords and in the mountains, both by day and during the white nights. At this time he would return again and again to questions of space and time and to a search for means of expressing them. Subsequently Gabo wrote in his realistic manifesto: "Look at our real space. What is it, if not continuous depth?"'

'These ideas, I believe, were evoked in him by the depth that he saw around him in the Norwegian fjords. He endeavoured to represent this depth in the things around us and frequently had recourse to effects obtained by applying the methods of reverse perspective, such as the ancient Byzantines used to render depth and movement. He spoke to me much about the meaning of line in sculpture, and that its function was not to delimit the boundaries of things but to show the trends of hidden rhythms and forces in them. Space and time, the infinity of the universe, the entire starry cosmos that surrounds us – these were the things that constantly excited him.'[1]

It was then, in the winter of 1915–16 and far away from the studios of Moscow, Munich and Paris, that Gabo began to make his first constructions, small figures and heads assembled from pieces of thin coloured cardboard pasted together to form intersecting planes. These constructions from the beginning were so precisely 'engineered' that the artist could afterwards reproduce them in more durable materials.

I do not wish to imply that these constructions sprang like Minerva from Gabo's brain free from preconceptions of any kind. The concept of an abstract art was being formulated in Munich at the very time that Gabo was there as a student. In 1908 the Piper Verlag had published Wilhelm Worringer's *Abstraction and Empathy* and four years later the same publisher was responsible for Kandinsky's *Concerning the Spiritual in Art*. These were seminal works in which the idea of a geometrical 'abstractive' art was first promulgated. Gabo did not read Kandinsky's book until about 1913 and Worringer's book much later, but the idea of abstraction was 'in the air'. Independently in Paris Cubism was developing towards abstraction, and when Gabo visited Paris in 1912 and 1913 he saw the works of Picasso, Braque, Gris, Laurens, Lipchitz, Duchamp-Villon and Archipenko. His brother Antoine was already in Paris at this time, but working more in the spirit of Vrubel, a Russian painter who manifested a tendency towards abstraction long before the Cubists (Gabo has paid tribute to him in his Mellon Lectures *On Divers Arts*). But Gabo was not satisfied with any of these experiments in abstraction, which in his opinion always stopped short of a proper understanding of form in space. 'The use of space in Cubism,' he declared, was 'unsystematic, accidental, in a sense anarchistic.' What Gabo demanded was 'a new kind of classicism, free in conception but disciplined in application'. What emerged from his meditations among the fjords of Norway was precisely a new kind of classicism.

This was to be defined in a manifesto which Gabo wrote on his return to Russia. At the outbreak of the Revolution (February 1917) Gabo and his brothers – Antoine had joined them in Oslo in December 1915 – decided at once to return home and reached Russia at the end of April 1917. The revolutionary ferment affected the arts no less than any other aspect of life in Moscow. The old Imperial Academy had been replaced by an organization called *Vkhutemas* (the Higher Art and Technical Workshop). Gabo himself has described this new institution:

'What is important to know about the character of the institution is that it was almost autonomous; it was both a school and a free academy where not only the current teaching of special professions was carried out ... but general discussions were held and seminars conducted amongst the students on diverse problems where the public could participate, and artists not officially on the faculty could speak and give lessons. ... During the seminars as well as during the general meetings, many ideological questions between opposing artists in our abstract group were thrashed out. These gatherings had a much greater influence on the later developments of constructive art than all the teaching.'[2]

To such discussions Gabo contributed the ideas he had evolved in the solitude of the Norwegian fjords, and these ideas were given their final formulation three years later in a *Realistic Manifesto* published on the occasion of a joint exhibition which he held with Antoine Pevsner – Pevsner signed the *Manifesto* but it was written by Gabo. Its central tenets were formulated as 'five fundamental principles', thus:

'The realization of our perceptions of the world in the forms of space and time is the only aim of our pictorial and plastic art.

In them we do not measure our works with the yardstick of beauty, we do not weigh them with pounds of tenderness and sentiments.

The plumb-line in our hand, eyes as precise as a ruler, in a spirit as taut as a compass . . . we construct our work as the universe constructs its own, as the engineer constructs his bridges, as the mathematician his formula of the orbits.

We know that everything has its own essential image; chair, table, lamp, telephone, book, house, man . . . they are all entire worlds with their own orbits.

That is why we in creating things take away from them the labels of their owners . . . all accidental and local, leaving only the reality of the constant rhythm of the forces in them.

1. Thence in painting we renounce colour as a pictorial element, colour is the idealized optical surface of objects; an exterior and superficial impression of them; colour is accidental and it has nothing in common with the innermost essence of a thing.

We affirm that the tone of a substance, i.e. its light-absorbing material body is its only pictorial reality.

2. We renounce in a line, its descriptive value; in real life there are no descriptive lines, description is an accidental trace of a man on things, it is not bound up with the essential life and constant structure of the body. Descriptiveness is an element of graphic illustration and decoration.

We affirm the line only as a direction of the static forces and their rhythm in objects.

3. We renounce volume as a pictorial and plastic form of space; one cannot measure space in volumes as one cannot measure liquid in yards; look at our space . . . what is it if not continuous depth?

We affirm depth as the only pictorial and plastic form of space.

4. We renounce in sculpture, the mass as a sculptural element. It is known to every engineer that the static forces of a solid body and its material strength do not depend on the quantity of the mass . . . example a rail, a T-beam, etc.

But you sculptors of all shades and directions, you still adhere to the age-old prejudice that you cannot free the volume of mass. Here (in this exhibition) we take four planes and we construct with them the same volume as of four tons of mass.

Thus we bring back to sculpture the line as a direction and in it we affirm depth as the one form of space.

5. We renounce the thousand-year-old delusion in art that held the static rhythms as the only elements of the plastic and pictorial arts.

We affirm in these arts a new element of the kinetic rhythms as the basic forms of our perceptions of real time.'[3]

I have quoted these principles in full because they contain everything essential for an understanding of Constructivism in general and of the work of Gabo in particular. Written nearly fifty years ago, they explain the nature of the art that Gabo still practises, and has practised consistently for half a century. Gabo himself has several essays of a later date and a whole volume of a confessional character (*On Divers Arts*, 1962) but he has never modified these principles formulated in 1920 'above the tempests of our weekdays. Across the ashes and cindered homes of the past. Before the gates of the vacant future.' Constructivism was born in the heart of the Russian Revolution, at the most decisive moment in the history of the modern world. It remains the most revolutionary doctrine of art ever pronounced in the modern world, as I shall now endeavour to explain. (*Plates 52, 53*)

I shall ignore on the present occasion the various modifications of or deviations from Constructivism represented by Tatlin, Rodchenko, the Stenbergs, Malevich and others (which have been fully described by Camilla Gray in *The Great Experiment: Russian Art 1863–1922*) to concentrate on the pure doctrine as represented by Gabo himself.

It will be seen that the key-word in Gabo's theory and practice of the art of sculpture is *Space*. This word has become the key-word of our civilization, and for this reason Gabo's perception of fifty years ago was prophetic. He was once asked in an interview by Abram Lassaw and Ilya Bolotowsky (1956) what in his opinion were the sources of this new concept of space in sculpture, and he replied:

'I would say that the real sources of the conception of space in sculpture are to be looked for in the whole state of our intellectual development and of the collective mind of our time. Space did not play a great role in the previous arts, not because the previous artists did not know anything about space, but because space represented to them only something which is there together with or attached to a mass volume. The volume and the material world around them was the main peg on which they hung their ideas and vision of the world. I would say that the philosophic events and the events in science at the beginning of this century have definitely made a crucial impact on the mentality of my generation. Whether many of us knew exactly what was going on in science, or not, does not really matter. The fact was that it was in the air, and an artist, with his sensitiveness, acts like a sponge. He may not know about it but he sucks in ideas and they work on him. On the other hand, we sculptors, rejecting the old sculpture, found its means insufficient for us to express our new images. We had to find new means and introduce new principles and that is why the principles of space and structure became basic. By doing my constructions I discovered the importance of space in them. We realized that every engineering object is, apart from its functional character, acting on us as an image.'[4]

This statement makes two assertions: that space as such has a special significance for 'the collective mind of our time', and that the sculptor of our time has to find new images to express this new, this special significance. We need not discuss the first of these assertions: it is sufficiently obvious to all of us that one of the distinguishing features of the modern epoch is that it has become far more conscious of space as such – that is to say, as the continuous extension in which we and all objects of perception exist. In a more general sense the Western artist has become increasingly conscious of space ever since Giotto first began to give the illusion of three-dimensionality to the figures in his paintings. But space as concept does not necessarily have reference to the existence of objects within it. Space is not necessarily 'a monolithic volume'; it can also be conceived as the continuum itself, as 'one continuous depth'. A construction can be made which represents space, not as a monolithic volume, but as a kinetic image of continuous extension. Such, at any rate, is the claim of Gabo, and all his work is to be experienced as such a kinetic image. The Constructive idea, he has said, has revealed a universal law, namely, 'that the elements of a visual art such as

lines, colours, shapes, possess their own forces of expression independent of any association with the external aspects of the world;
that their life and their action are self-conditioned psychological
phenomena rooted in human nature; that those elements (lines,
colours, shapes) are not chosen by convention for any utilitarian
or other reason as words and figures are, they are not merely
abstract signs, but they are immediately and organically bound
up with human emotions'.[5]

This is clear enough as the statement of a theory of art distinct
from Cubism, abstraction or any other theory of modern art.
Indeed, it represents a radically new approach to art itself, and
that is why Gabo prefers to speak of Constructivism rather than
of Sculpture. All previous conceptions of art have involved
representations of the external aspect of the world, or have taken
external aspects of the world as a point of departure (most non-
figurative art has a 'kernel' of this kind). Gabo dared to conceive
the independent existence of a work of art, deprived of all
naturalistic content or inspiration, existing solely as an image of
impersonal forces, but not thereby evading emotional responses
when presented to a human being and perceived as an image.
Indeed, one might attribute to such images the power of evoking
in some degree the Pascalian *frisson*: 'Le silence éternel de ces
espaces infinies m'effraie.'

Gabo has said that the constructive idea sees and values art
only as a creative act. 'By creative act it means every material or
spiritual work which is destined to stimulate or perfect the substance of material or spiritual life.' This is essentially Plato's conception of the function of art: the work of art is an embodiment
of the physical laws of the universe, which are harmonic in their
nature, and in virtue of this representative function, the work of
art is capable of modifying man's environment and of transmitting this harmony to his soul. But it only has this power by
virtue of its universal, abstract perfection. When the work of
art becomes 'a mirror of perfection', mankind is then given a
model to which his spirit can conform. The ultimate aim is to
create a complete civic environment which will then inevitably
have this function; in the words of the Realistic Manifesto: 'In
the squares and on the streets we are placing our work convinced

that art must not remain a sanctuary for the idle, a consolation for the weary, and a justification for the lazy. Art should attend us everywhere that life flows and acts . . . at the bench, at the table, at work, at rest, at play; on working days and holidays . . . at home and on the road . . . in order that the flame to live should not extinguish in mankind.' Or in the words Plato used to express the same ideal: 'We must look for those craftsmen who by the happy gift of nature are capable of following the trail of true beauty and grace, that our young men, dwelling as it were in a salubrious region, may receive benefit from all things about them, whence the influence that emanates from works of beauty may waft itself to eye or ear like a breeze that brings from wholesome places health, and so from earliest childhood insensibly guide them to likeness, to friendship, to harmony with beautiful reason.'[6]

'Works that express harmony with beautiful reason' is as near as we can get to a definition of Gabo's constructions, and it is for that reason that I have called his work classical – it might be more exact to call it Platonic. He has not been alone in this conception of art – with modifications it was the conception held not only by his brother Antoine, but also by Malevich and Mondrian, and generally by the Dutch *de Stijl* group. But Gabo has realized the conception with greatest consistency and purity, and his work in its totality is not only an impressive witness to a life of high endeavour, but points even more impressively to the art of the future. 'Today is the deed. We will account for it tomorrow.'

The foregoing consideration of constructivism in general and of Gabo's art in particular has apparently led to a contradiction that cannot be evaded. I have implied throughout this book that creative activity offers the only possibility of resolving the spiritual disease of alienation. Perhaps too often I have assumed that the reconciliation of man and nature, of psyche and self, is an organic process, that is to say, a process intimately related to the vital impulse in 'being' or existence itself. The abstract or Platonic ideal of form seems at first to contradict this vitalist assumption, but not on deeper consideration of the function of form in nature. As I once said in a preface to a volume that discussed all aspects of the problem of form,[7] 'the revelation that perception itself is essentially a pattern-selecting and pattern-making function; that pattern is inherent in the physical structure or in the functioning of the nervous system; that matter itself analyses into coherent patterns or arrangements of molecules; and the gradual realization that all these patterns are effective and ontologically significant by virtue of an organization of their parts which can only be characterized as *aesthetic* – all this development has brought works of art and natural phenomena on to an identical plane of enquiry. Aesthetics is no longer an isolated science of beauty; science can no longer neglect aesthetic factors.' This statement was confirmed by the several scientists who contributed to the volume and the general conclusion to be drawn from them (and the general conclusion to this present volume) is that there is no distinction to be made between organic form and what in aesthetics we call 'pure' form. According to one of the contributors to *Aspects of Form* (the biologist A. M. Dalcq), 'whatever aspect of form is examined, be it in the most general sense, or in morphogenesis, in evolution, or in mental achievements, the primacy of an Order, of an Idea, can always be asserted'. That, too, has been the discovery of every significant modern artist, from Cézanne to Gabo. Science and art, in their deepest researches, have one and the same aim, the desire and pursuit of wholeness or unity.

Note

'The Function of the Arts in Contemporary Society' and the essay on Henry Moore were originally written for UNESCO and are reprinted with permission. 'The Limits of Painting' was originally delivered as an address to the IV Corso Internazionale d'Alta Cultura (1962) at the Cini Foundation, Venice. 'Rational Society and Irrational Art' was a contribution to a volume in honour of Herbert Marcuse (Boston, Beacon Press, 1967). 'Style and Expression' is an enlarged version of an Introduction to *The Styles of European Art* (London, Thames and Hudson, 1965). The essays on Hieronymus Bosch and Vermeer are revised versions of introductions contributed to 'The Masters', a series of volumes published by Knowledge Publications, London. The essay on Kandinsky was first published as an introduction to a volume in the Faber Gallery (London, Faber and Faber, 1959). 'The Sculpture of Matisse' was originally written for the catalogue of the Henri Matisse Retrospective of 1966, organized by the University of California Art Council and Art Galleries, and subsequently published in book form by the University of California Press. The essay on Ben Nicholson was written for a French publisher, but I have no record of its publication. 'Naum Gabo' was the introduction to the catalogue of the retrospective exhibition held at the Tate Gallery in March, 1966. The essay on Vincent van Gogh has not previously been published. All these essays have been subjected to varying degrees of revision and extension.

H. R.

Text References

INTRODUCTION

1. (p. 9), From a review in the *Burlington Magazine*, May 1934
2. (p. 10), *Last Lectures*. Cambridge, 1939, pp. 23–4
3. (p. 10), *On Modern Art*. English edition, London, 1945, p. 53

I THE FUNCTION OF THE ARTS IN CONTEMPORARY SOCIETY

1. (p. 16), Werner Jaeger, *Paideia*. Oxford, 1947, vol. III, p. 161
2. (p. 17), Matthew Arnold, *Lectures and Essays in Criticism*. Ed. R. H. Super, University of Michigan Press, 1962, pp. 120–1
3. (p. 18), Cf. Otto von Simson, *The Gothic Cathedral*, New York, 1965. The phrase quoted comes from this work (p. 62)
4. (p. 20), Jakob Burckhardt, *Reflec-tions on History*. Trans. by M. D. Hottinger. London, 1943, p. 179
5. (p. 22), *Op. cit.*, p. 179
6. (p. 23), T. S. Eliot, *Notes Towards the Definition of Culture*. London, 1948, p. 120
7. (p. 25), *Op. cit.*, p. 260
8. (p. 25), *Ibid.*, p. 261
9. (p. 27) Burckhardt, *op. cit.*, pp. 85–6
10. (p. 28), *The Prelude*, XI (1850), 105–21

II RATIONAL SOCIETY AND IRRATIONAL ART

1. (p. 30), The quotations in this paragraph come from pp. 61–4 of *One-Dimensional Man*, New York and London, 1964
2. (p. 30), *Surrealism*. London, 1936. Reprinted in *The Philosophy of Modern Art*. London and New York, 1952
3. (p. 31), Donald Davie in *The New Statesman*
4. (p. 31), I was once told by a member of an audience I was addressing in Zagreb, Jugoslavia, that my remarks were incomprehensible to him because man in a communist economy does not suffer from *Angst*. That was before an earthquake had destroyed his city
5. (p. 32), *Schriften zum Theater*. Berlin and Frankfurt, 1957, p. 63
6. (p. 32), Eric Bentley, *The Life of the Drama*, 1965, p. 163
7. (p. 32), Quoted from Brecht's 'Prospectus of the Diderot Society' by Bentley, p. 162

8. (p. 33), *Op. cit.*, p. 67

9. (p. 36), *The Hidden God: A Study of Tragic Vision in the Pensées of Pascal and the Tragedies of Racine.* Trans. by Philip Thody. London, 1964, p. 60.

For 'clarity' in this passage we may substitute Coleridge's 'unity' or Valéry's 'form'.

10. (p. 38), *One-Dimensional Man*, pp. 248–9

III THE LIMITS OF PAINTING

1. (p. 40), Michael Sullivan, *An Introduction to Chinese Art.* London, 1961, pp. 98–9; Mai-Mai Sze, *The Tao of Painting.* New York, 1956, pp. 46–51. Both authors quote other authorities, such as Alexander Soper and Arthur Waley

2. (p. 43), *Some T'ang and Pre-T'ang Texts on Painting*, Leiden, 1954. I take the story from Sullivan, *op. cit.*, p. 99

3. (p. 43), Cf. *Muntu: an Outline of Neo-African Culture*, by Janheinz Jahn. London, 1958.

4. (p. 44), From 'My Painting', written by Jackson Pollock and published in *Possibilities I.* New York, Winter 1947–8

5. (p. 44), Bryan Robertson, *Jackson Pollock.* London, 1960, p. 91

6. (p. 46), Georges Limbour has indicated its 'fatal flaw'—'On n'a pas assez remarqué la facheuse tendance du Surréalisme à ce qui est le contraire de la poésie: le scientisme.' Preface to *André Masson: Entretiens avec Georges Charbonnier.* Paris, 1958

7. (p. 48), *Anatomy of My Universe*, III

8. (p. 49), *Anatomy*, V

9. (p. 50), D. T. Suzuki, *Zen and Japanese Culture.* New York, 1959, p. 17

10. (p. 50), Cf. *Zen for the West* by William Barrett. Introduction to *Zen Buddhism* by D. T. Suzuki. New York, 1956

11. (p. 50), *Entretiens*, p. 149

12. (p. 50), *Ibid.*, p. 122

13. (p. 51), *Entretiens*, pp. 122–5

14. (p. 51), Georges Duthuit, 'Où allez-vous Miró'. *Cahiers d'Art.* No. 8–10, 1936, p. 262, Cf. *Joan Miró*, by James Thrall Soby. New York, 1959, p. 28

15. (p. 51), Interview with James Johnson Sweeney, 'Joan Miró: Comment and Interview'. *Partisan Review*, No. 2, 1948, p. 210. Quoted by James Thrall Soby, *op. cit.*, p. 100

16. (p. 53), From the answer to a questionnaire written by Jackson Pollock and published in *Arts and Architecture*, vol. lxi, February, 1944

17. (p. 55), James K. Feibleman, 'Concreteness in Painting: Abstract Expressionism and After'. *The Personalist*, vol. 43, no. 1. Winter 1962. Published by the University of Southern California, U.S.A.

IV STYLE AND EXPRESSION

1. (p. 58), *Kunstgeschichtliche Grundbegriffe*, translated as *Principles of Art History*, London, 1932

2. (p. 61), Nikolaus Pevsner & Michael Meier, *Grünewald*. London, 1958

3. (p. 62), His *Mörder Hoffnung der*

Frauen, the series of drawings he made to illustrate his play of that name, has been described as follows: 'this drama of love, confusion and murder, this struggle between man and woman for love's sake, is as barbarous, passionate and nauseating

as that of Siegfried & Brunhild. Since the days of the Nibelungen no such devastating passions have been represented in German art. Kokoschka introduced yet another perversion: that of love coupled with the lust for blood.' (Edith Hoffman, *Kokoschka: Life and Work.*, London, 1947, p. 56
4. (p. 64), Otto Benesch, *Edvard Munch.* London, 1960, p. 30
5. (p. 69), E. H. Gombrich, *Art and Illusion: a Study in the Psychology of*
Pictorial Representation. London, 1960
6. (p. 74), Quoted from *Art and Visual Perception: a psychology of the creative eye.* By Rudolf Arnheim. University of California Press, 1954. My italics
7. (p. 75), *The Life of Forms.* Trans. C. B. Hogan and G. Kubler. New York, 1948, p. 44
8. (p. 76), Oxford University Press, 1925, pp. 35–6

VII VINCENT VAN GOGH: A STUDY IN ALIENATION

1. (p. 94), *Transformations*, p. 187. I have adopted the growing practice of calling Van Gogh by his first name —it avoids the difficulty which most non-Dutch people experience in pronouncing Van Gogh, and there are many precedents for the liberty in the history of art
2. (p. 94), *Psychiatrische en Neuro-*
logische Bladen (Ps. and N. Bulletin), 1941, No. 5. Trans. of the main points of this article are given in *The Complete Letters of Vincent Van Gogh*, London and New York, 3 vols. Vol. 3, pp. 605–9
3. (p. 96), *Letters*, III, no. 596
4. (p. 105), *Letters*, III, no. 554.

VIII THE SCULPTURE OF MATISSE: BALANCE, PURITY, SERENITY

1. (p. 110), *Henri Matisse.* Texts by Jean Leymarie, Herbert Read, William S. Liebermann. University of California Press, 1966, p. 25
2. (p. 111), 'Notes of a Painter', 1908. Trans. by Margaret Scolari. From *Matisse: his Art and his Public*, by Alfred H. Barr, Jr., New York, 1951, pp. 120–1
3. (p. 112), Barr, *op. cit.*, p. 40 (my italics). Another translation is given in Raymond Escholier, *Matisse from the Life.* Trans. Geraldine and H. M. Colville. London, 1960, p. 48
4. (p. 113), Barr, *op. cit.*, p. 52
5. (p. 113), Escholier, *op. cit.*, p. 138
6. (p. 114), Escholier, *op. cit.*, p. 141 (my italics)
7. (p. 116), Barr, *op. cit.*, Appendix A, pp. 550–2
8. (p. 117), Barr, *op. cit.*, p. 94
9. (p. 118), *Ibid*, p. 100
10. (p. 118), Gertrude Stein, *The Autobiography of Alice B. Toklas.* New York, 1933, pp. 77–8
11. (p. 118), Georges Duthuit, *The Fauvist Painters.* Trans. Ralph Manheim. New York, 1950, p. 93
12. (p. 118), Ludwig Munz and Viktor Löwenfeld, *Die plastische Arbeiten Blinder.* Brunn, 1934
Viktor Löwenfeld, *The Nature of Creative Activity.* London, 1939
13. (p. 118), Duthuit, *op. cit.*, p. 62 (Duthuit's italics)
14. (p. 120), This information has

been obtained from Marguerite Duthuit and Jean Matisse, based on their comprehensive files from the casting establishment, and on their own complete files of exhibitions
15. (p. 122), Jean Selz, *Modern Sculpture, Origins and Evolutions*. Trans. by

Annette Michelson. London, 1963, pp. 189, 192
16. (p. 122), Barr, *op. cit.*, pp. 119–23 (my italics). Henri Matisse, 'Notes of a Painter' originally published *La Grande Revue*. Paris, 25 December 1908

IX HENRY MOORE: THE RECONCILING ARCHETYPE

1. (p. 123), Herbert Read, *Henry Moore, Life and Work*. London, 1965
2. (p. 124), Erich Neumann, *The Archetypal World of Henry Moore*. New York, 1959
3. (p. 124), C. G. Jung, *Collected Works*. vol. 15 ('The Spirit in Man in Art and Literature'), p. 162. New York, 1966
4. (p. 127), T. E. Hulme, *Speculations*. London, 1924
5. (p. 127), Wilhelm Worringer,

Form in Gothic. London, 1927
6. (p. 131), Kenneth Clark, *The Nude: a Study in Ideal Form*. New York, 1956, p. 25
7. (p. 131), Sigmund Freud, *The Ego and the Id*. Trans. Joan Riviere. London, 1927, pp. 55–6
8. (p. 132), K. Clark, *op. cit.*, pp. 256–9
9. (p. 135), C. G. Jung, *op. cit.*, p. 322
10. (p. 136), Erich Neumann, *The Great Mother*. New York, 1955

X THE LUCID ORDER OF WASSILY KANDINSKY

1. (p. 139), Cologne, 1958; London, 1959
2. (p. 142), First German edition, Munich, 1908. English translation by Michael Bullock, London, 1953
3. (p. 146), London, 1947
4. (p. 149), Cf. Jean Arp: "Kandinsky told me that his grandfather had come

trotting into Russia on the back of a small charger that was spangled with bells, arriving from one of those enchanted Asiatic mountains all made of porcelain. There is no doubt that this grandfather had bequeathed deep secrets to Kandinsky.' *Wassily Kandinsky*, by Max Bill. Paris, 1951

XII NAUM GABO: BEFORE THE GATES OF THE VACANT FUTURE

1. (p. 157), Alexei Pevsner: *Naum Gabo and Antoine Pevsner*. Amsterdam, 1964, pp. 13–14
2. (p. 158), *Gabo: Constructions, Sculpture, Paintings, Drawings*. London, 1957, p. 152
3. (p. 160), *Ibid.*, p. 152
4. (p. 161), *Ibid.*, pp. 159–60

5. (p. 162), *The Constructive Idea in Art* (1937). *Ibid.*, p. 163
6. (p. 163), *Republic, III*, 401. Trans. Paul Shorey, Loeb Library
7. (p. 164), *Aspects of Form: a Symposium on Form in Nature and Art*. Ed. by Lancelot Law Whyte. London, 1951

List of Illustrations

35 Henri Matisse
Head of Jeanette V, 1910
Bronze h. 58 cms
Museum of Modern Art, New York
Photo Soichi Sunami

36 Henri Matisse
Back I, 1909
Bronze h. 188 cms
Tate Gallery, London

37 Henri Matisse
Back II, 1913
Bronze h. 187 cms
Tate Gallery, London

38 Henri Matisse
Back III, 1914–17
Bronze h. 186·5 cms
Tate Gallery, London

39 Henri Matisse
Back IV, 1930
Bronze h. 188 cms
Tate Gallery, London

40 Henri Matisse
Tiari with Necklace, 1930
Bronze h. 20·5 cms
Cone Collection, Baltimore Museum of Art

41 Michelangelo
Rondanini Pietà, until 1555–64
Marble h. 195 cms
Castello Sforzeco, Milan

42 Henry Moore
Mother and Child, 1931
Verde di Prato h. 20·5 cms
Collection Michael Maclagan, Oxford
Photo Henry Moore

43 Henry Moore
Mother and Child, 1938
Elmwood h. 91·5 cms
Museum of Modern Art, New York
Photo Henry Moore

44 Henry Moore
Two Women with Children in a Shelter, 1941

Watercolour and pen 38 × 48·5 cms
Private Collection
Photo Henry Moore

45 Henry Moore
Relief No. 1, 1959
Bronze h. 223·5 cms
Opera House, Berlin
Photo Henry Moore

46 Henry Moore
Helmet Head, No. 2, 1950
Bronze h. 35·5 cms
Private Collection
Photo Lidbrooke

47 Wassily Kandinsky
Improvisation 35, 1914
Oil on canvas 110·5 × 120 cms
Offentliche Kunstammlung, Basle

48 Wassily Kandinsky
Green Accent, No. 623, 1935
Oil on canvas 81·5 × 100 cms
The Solomon R. Guggenheim Museum, New York

49 Wassily Kandinsky
Black Accompaninent, 1924
Oil on canvas 166 × 135 cms
Collection Galerie Maeght, Paris

50 Wassily Kandinsky
Each for Itself, 1934
Oil and tempera on canvas 60 × 70 cms
Collection Nina Kandinsky, Paris

51 Ben Nicholson
Torre del Grillo, Rome, 1955
Drawing
Photo by Studio St Ives Ltd

52 Naum Gabo
Bronze Spheric Theme, c. 1960
Phosphor bronze h. 97 cms
Collection Miriam Gabo

53 Naum Gabo
Linear Construction, No. 2, 1949/53
Plastic h. 92 cms
Collection Miriam Gabo
Photo John Webb

Index